HELPING
YOUR
HANDICAPPED
CHILD

HELPING YOUR HANDICAPPED CHILD

George W. Paterson

RELIGION AND MEDICINE SERIES

Glen W. Davidson, Editor

AUGSBURG PUBLISHING HOUSE
MINNEAPOLIS, MINNESOTA

I am most grateful to the parents who generously shared their experience with me in tape-recorded interviews and so made this book possible. In keeping with my promise of confidentiality to them, none of the children or parents mentioned in the book is referred to by their actual name.

HELPING YOUR HANDICAPPED CHILD

Copyright © 1975 Augsburg Publishing House

Library of Congress Catalog Card No. 74-14185

International Standard Book No. 0-8066-1467-6

Scripture quotations unless otherwise noted are from the Revised Standard Version of the Bible, copyright 1946, 1952, and 1971 by the Division of Christian Education of the National Council of Churches.

Manufactured in the United States of America

Contents

Foreword

"Your child is handicapped." No parent wants to hear that diagnosis. Unfortunately, thousands of parents every year do hear that their child has mental retardation, cerebral palsy, deafness, blindness, cleft palate, incomplete limb formation, or some other birth defect. More crippling than birth defects, however, may be the parents' unresolved feelings of shock, anger, guilt, or grief that affect the way they can relate to their infant. Almost any child can respond and learn despite a handicap. But how can a child grow with parental rejection, whether that rejection be intentional or unwitting? All children with some handicap can be helped to utilize their abilities, but not when they are deprived of encouragement and love.

George Paterson has written this book to help parents of handicapped children meet the demands of a very "special kind of parenthood." He translates the technical terminology of medicine into the language of laymen, particularly those parents who seek to interpret their experience within a framework of religion. He helps parents distinguish between false hopes and realistic courage. For those parents who live under fears of making mistakes, Dr. Paterson suggests ways of meeting a child's needs for love, discipline, and training. He raises the tough questions many parents must face: "What should we do?" "What can we tell our friends?" "Can we find help we can afford?"

7

In health crisis, we often wrestle with questions "Why?" "Why did this happen?" "Why did it happen *to us?*" "Who is responsible?" Some of these questions can be answered, but we suffer intensely when they cannot be or are not answered. It doesn't often occur to us that our questions may seek more to relieve us of feelings than obtain factual data for us. Yet many of the questions asked by parents of handicapped children are feelings of guilt and bewilderment. And their suffering is made all the more intense by the expectation that someone, somehow, must be held accountable for the handicap. Perhaps the strongest part of the book is Dr. Paterson's examination of this kind of suffering.

This book is a part of a series designed to treat health problems with religious insight and medical accuracy. It is based on a study Dr. Paterson conducted to determine needs of parents with cerebral palsied children. Dr. Paterson received his doctorate upon completion of the study in 1969, and since then has been both a chaplain and researcher at the University of Iowa Hospitals and Clinics. He is the father of four children, has been both a pastor and campus chaplain, and presently holds academic appointments in the College of Medicine and the School of Religion of The University of Iowa.

Glen W. Davidson, Ph.D.
Director, Division of Medical Humanities
Southern Illinois University
School of Medicine

HELPING YOUR HANDICAPPED CHILD

1

What
Happened . . . ?

. . . to Bret

Bret Holloway is a blond, blue-eyed, active, healthy three-and-a-half-year-old whose hearing is severely impaired. Although his parents suspected for some time that something was wrong, they did not know for certain what it was until Bret was past two. At first they thought him simply inattentive. His mother noticed that he would not respond when she would call him from another room until she came into the room where he was. She noticed too that when he woke up from his nap and began to cry for her, she could not quiet him unless she came into the room where he could see her. Although he began walking shortly after his first birthday, Bret was not beginning to form words as had his older brother and sister at that age. "He's just a slow talker," grandmother said. But by the time his second birthday had come around, Bret was still not speaking.

By this time the Holloways were seriously concerned. They were beginning to suspect that he was mentally retarded. Bret's mother had read about "autistic" children, and wondered if perhaps he was a victim of this strange emotional disorder. They expressed their fears to their pediatrician, who performed a hearing test as part of his examination of Bret and then referred them to an audiologist for a more complete

11

evaluation of Bret's hearing. The audiologist confirmed the physician's report: Bret does have a severe hearing loss. Like most other children with this problem, he is not "totally" deaf; he does possess some residual capacity for hearing. However, there is no medical or surgical treatment which offers any possibility of significant improvement for Bret's hearing. He will have to learn to live with this condition, and his parents will have to help him adapt to his handicap.

One of the first recommendations was that Bret be fitted with a hearing aid and that he be taught how to use it, for hearing is learned, not innate. The Holloways were also told that Bret would need special training in order to develop language and speech. The first year of life is a crucial time in this process, and Bret was delayed because of his inability to hear. Bret will need to be taught to read speech by observing facial movements, because even with his hearing aid he will still have considerable hearing loss. When he starts to school, he will probably need to attend a special school, or at least special classes, for the deaf. Later on, when the delay in his development has been overcome, he may be able to transfer to a regular school.

One of the first questions Bret's parents asked their doctor was, "What caused this problem? Was there something we could have done to prevent it?" They were told that many different things can cause congenital or early childhood deafness. Among them are infections which may damage the fetus before birth, such as rubella ("German measles") during the first three months of pregnancy. Other possible causes include blood incompatibilities, injury at the time of birth as a result of difficult labor or delivery, prematurity, and the failure of the new-born to breathe immediately. They also learned that deafness may result from a hereditary malformation of the auditory nerve or of the inner or middle ear. Although the cause of Bret's deafness has not been definitely established, their doctor believes it is related to the fact that Bret was born six weeks premature.

Bret's mother and father have also discovered that their son's handicap is not as rare as they had imagined. There are almost 39,000 children enrolled in schools for the deaf in the United States, and it is estimated that an additional 216,000 children of school age need special educational help because of hearing problems.

The Holloways know that they will have to play a very active role in Bret's training and development if he is to learn to accept and overcome his handicap. Already he has been fitted with the recommended hearing aid and wears it continuously. His parents are trying to introduce him to the world of sound which most of us take so much for granted. They are careful to keep him in a normal environment where he is exposed to sound and speech all day long: They are teaching him to recognize such things as the roar of a crowd at a football game, the noise of a jet airliner taking off, the rhythms of a marching band. They are also teaching him to hear and recognize words by speaking close to his ear, very distinctly, and by repeating the same sounds frequently. They are careful that he can see their faces when they speak to him, so that he can learn to associate words with movements of the lips and face. In this, they have the guidance of an otologist (a physician who specializes in the treatment of the ear) and a special education teacher trained in problems of speech and hearing.

They have already recognized how much Bret's development has been delayed by his deafness. They know that this delay will take some time to overcome. Although Bret has had his hearing aid for more than a year now, he is just beginning to talk, and many of his words are indistinct or imperfectly formed. Since the deaf child learns more slowly than the child with normal hearing, Bret's educational progress will be slower than that of other children. It may require two or more years for him to progress from first to second grade level, and another year-and-a-half or two to complete third grade work. At one time, it was commonly assumed that deaf children were usually mentally retarded. Now that more appropriate tests have been devised for the non-hearing, it appears that intelligence is distributed as normally among the deaf as it is among the hearing. There is no indication at this time that Bret suffers from mental retardation.

Bret may also have some emotional problems as a consequence of his hearing loss. Although there is no such thing as a "deaf personality," the deaf child does experience some particular kinds of stress related to his handicap. As a result, he is apt to be less mature socially and emotionally, and to have more emotional conflicts than the child with normal hearing. Perhaps two key words in understanding these stresses are *frustration* and *isolation*. The child with a hearing loss experiences more than his share of both as a result of his difficulty in mastering the innumerable and constantly recurring tasks which involve spoken communication between persons.

All of this means that it will require enormous patience and understanding on the part of Bret's parents to accept his handicap, and to *help him accept it,* without clinging to unrealistic expectations on the one hand, or on the other, being overcome by discouragement. Together they will have to strive to maximize his potential—physical, intellectual, social, emotional, spiritual—to the fullest possible extent. They will need considerable help in this, from physicians, special education teachers, counselors, and perhaps from their pastor. They will also need the understanding and support of their family, friends, and neighbors. One of the most difficult aspects of Bret's handicap is its invisibility. Bret looks so "normal"— yet he functions very differently from a "normal"—i.e., hearing—child.

. . . to Tammy

Tammy Nelson is seven years old. She attends a special class for trainable mentally retarded children. She has the rather flattened face, the small, slanting eyes, the large tongue and short neck characteristic of Down's syndrome (also known as mongolism). It was such physical characteristics as these, along with a pronounced lack of muscle tone, that enabled a pediatrician to diagnose Tammy's condition shortly after birth. The doctor informed her mother and father of the diagnosis before they took her home from the hospital; later on they had her examined by another specialist who confirmed their own doctor's judgment. Both doctors were careful to emphasize to Tammy's parents that there is no cure or treatment available for mongolism, and that Tammy's handicap is not one that they have unwittingly caused, or that they could have prevented.

An estimated 60,000 persons in the United States are afflicted with Down's syndrome, which occurs about three times in every 1000 live births. It is caused by various kinds of chromosomal abnormalities. Persons with the most common type have an extra 21st chromosome instead of the usual pair, or a total of 47 instead of 46 chromosomes. For some reason, the defect occurs much more often when the mother is over 35 years of age; more than half such births occur to women over 40. Tammy's mother was 38 when she was born; her other three children, all boys, had been normal in every respect. If she had been under 35, chromosome studies would have been carried out to determine the type of mongolism and the probability that it would occur in future children. However, since Mrs. Nelson is in the older age group, her physician assumes that Tammy's mongolism is the "regular" type, and the risk of its recurrence in future births is the same as that for any mother of comparable age (under 35 years, 1 in 150 births; over 40, 1 in 40 births). Because of their age and the fact that they already have four children, Tammy's parents have decided not to have any more children.

Tammy was smaller at birth than her brothers had been; moreover, she was very slow to gain weight during her first year. Feeding was a constant problem, for she had difficulty in swallowing and in learning to chew, and she quickly became tired while being fed. As a baby she was very quiet and slept a great deal. When she did awake, she appeared somewhat apathetic and weak; the doctor told her mother this was because Tammy's nervous system was immature in comparison to that of normal children. Her resistance to colds has always been low, and she has one frequently; she has also had to be treated occasionally for eye infections.

Her development has been markedly slower than that of her brothers. She did not sit up until shortly after her first birthday, nor begin to crawl until she was a year-and-a-half old. She was past three before she was walking; generally her movements are awkward, clumsy, and uncoordinated. She did not begin to form words until about a year after she began to walk, and it is still rather difficult at times for persons who do not know her to understand her.

However, she has been and continues to be a very lovable child, who responds readily to interest, affection, tenderness. She tends to be rather placid, not easily roused to anger, and she plays well with other children. On the other hand, she can be quite stubborn, especially when it is necessary to depart from her regular daily routine, for she is unable to shift rapidly from one object or situation to another. She is an artful mimic, and this has proved helpful in teaching her to master many of the activities of daily life. Although she is somewhat near-sighted, her hearing is good and she is quite fond of music, especially if it has strong rhythm.

What can Tammy's parents expect for her future development? They know that her mental capacity is quite limited, and that she will probably never progress beyond the level of a six- or seven-year-old normal child. Although her memory is good, and she will acquire a fair speaking and listening vocabulary, it is doubtful that she will ever learn to read. Her mastery of arithmetic will probably never be sufficient that she can be trusted to handle money. Although she is not able to attend regular school classes, Tammy is capable of benefitting from special training for persons of her mental capacity. The primary goal of her education is to help her develop practical skills in activities of daily living. She will be able to help her parents with tasks around the home such as washing, ironing, cleaning, caring for pets; if they lived in a rural area there might be outdoor tasks which she could perform with much satisfaction.

The Nelsons know that Tammy's life expectancy is shorter than average. About half of the children born with Down's syndrome also have congenital heart defects, and leukemia occurs three times as frequently among them as among other persons. Nevertheless, Tammy may live well into adulthood, and her parents are wondering whether it may eventually be necessary to place her in a home or institution for mentally retarded persons. When she is twenty, they will be nearing sixty, and may find it increasingly difficult to care for her at home. However, they want to keep her with them as long as possible, for they know she needs the warmth and affection they can give her, and they enjoy the love she is able to give them in return. She has demanded a great deal of time, patience, and understanding from them, and it has been difficult at times not to neglect Tammy's brothers in their concern for her special needs. Nevertheless, they have experienced many rewards in their task of parenthood, and they realize that if the time comes that it is necessary for her to leave their home, it will be difficult for them as well as for her.

. . . to Jennifer

When Jennifer Albright was fifteen months old, her parents were told that she had cerebral palsy. Although this information was painful to them, it came as no surprise, for they had suspected for months that something was not right with their first child. Almost from the beginning, Jennifer had been a difficult child to feed, especially when they started her on solid foods. She also seemed to be much slower than their friends' children in achieving those things that give parents so much pride—rolling over, sitting up, crawling, beginning to form words. Even now, at two-and-a-half years, Jennifer is not able to walk or even stand alone. When the Albrights took her to their family doctor for her six months' examination, they mentioned their fears to him. He reassured them that she appeared to be normal and healthy, and that she was probably just slow in developing. However, when she was a year old, he referred them to a pediatrician in a nearby city. This physician examined Jennifer, told the Albrights that she had cerebral palsy, and referred them again to an educational and rehabilitation center for the treatment of handicapped children.

Of necessity, Jennifer's parents have learned a good deal about the term "cerebral palsy." They know that it refers to a condition of paralysis, weakness, or lack of coordination resulting from damage to the motor control centers of the brain which takes place before, during, or shortly after birth. They know too that their daughter is one of some 14,000 such children born each year in the United States, and that approximately one in seven does not survive infancy. The causes of cerebral palsy are so numerous that the specific cause of a particular child's handicap is often difficult to establish. Among them are infections which may be suffered by the mother during pregnancy or by the newborn child itself: rubella would be an example of the former; meningitis and encephalitis, of the latter. Injuries suffered by the fetus before birth, or by the newborn during prolonged or difficult delivery may also cause cerebral palsy, and such factors as prematurity or Rh-factor incompatibility may be responsible for the handicap. One common denominator among many different causes may be lack of oxygen supply to the brain, for the brain requires more oxygen than other body tissues in order to function and can be permanently damaged through deprivation. In Jennifer's case, the cause of the handicap remains unknown. However, the physicians have assured her mother and father that it is unlikely that they either caused or could have prevented the damage which has left her disabled.

The Albrights have learned that there are a number of different types of cerebral palsy, designated by such terms as *spacticity, athetosis, rigidity, ataxia, tremor,* and *atonia.* Jennifer's handicap is classified as *spastic quadriplegia.* The term *spastic* refers to the tendency of her muscles to over-react. When her arm is extended, for example, the opposing muscles pull it back in a "clasp-knife" type of reaction. This results in contractures which pull her hands and feet into distorted positions—her hand bent against her forearm, her legs with a tendency to "scissor." The term *quadriplegia* indicates that all four of her limbs are involved. In some cases, only one arm or leg is affected; in others, the legs only, or an arm and a leg on only one side of the body.

Persons who suffer from cerebral palsy are also often subject to other, related handicaps. About half are moderately retarded mentally, with IQs in the range of 50–90; many have vision or hearing defects; and convulsions are not uncommon, nor are various disorders of thinking, perception, and behavior. At the present time Jennifer's handicap appears to be limited to her neuromotor impairment; however, this does affect her speech, and she will require considerable help in overcoming this handicap.

Jennifer's parents are comforted by the realization that the damage to her brain will not get any worse as she grows older. However, they also understand that it can neither be cured nor corrected. Yet even though the underlying injury cannot be remedied, Jennifer can be helped considerably through a long-range, comprehensive rehabilitation program, extending over many years and involving a wide range of specialists. In addition to the pediatrician already mentioned, they may at one time or another need the help of an orthopedist, physiatrist, neurologist, psychiatrist, opthalmologist, otolaryngologist—as well as that of such non-medical specialists as a clinical psychologist, physical therapist, occupational therapist, speech therapist, special education teacher, rehabilitation counselor, social worker, and clergyman.

Already Jennifer has been fitted with braces at the rehabilitation center to which her parents were referred, and a physical therapist has started her on a daily program of exercises designed to strengthen her muscles and improve her control of them. Her parents are responsible for seeing that these exercises are done regularly, even though some of them are rather painful and Jennifer often objects. Later on, it may be possible to correct some of her deformities and improve her muscle function and skill through surgery. However, her parents have been warned not to expect any surgical "miracles," but only limited improvement. She will also need occupational therapy as she grows older to help her master those activities of daily living which other children learn in the normal course of development: feeding and dressing herself, toileting, cleanliness, writing. Speech therapy will also play an important role in Jennifer's development, as we have noted.

Already her parents are wondering what the future holds for their daughter. How seriously will her handicap impair her, to what extent will it prevent her from living a "normal" life? Will she be able to attend a regular school? How far will she be able to progress in school? Will it be possibe for her to hold a job, or will she be financially dependent on them the rest of her life? What about marriage—will she be able someday to have her own home and family? Most of the goals we hold for a "normal" child are doubtful for Jennifer. As yet, the Albrights have many more questions than answers.

The professionals who work with them have encouraged them to take a cautious attitude toward many of these questions, to "wait and see." They do not want to foreclose prematurely on some area of Jennifer's development and thus impose unnecessary limitations on her. On the other hand, they do not want Jennifer or her parents to live with the burden of expectations that are unrealistic or even impossible.

What about the social and emotional consequences of a handicap such as Jennifer's? Investigators do not believe that there is a typical "cerebral palsy personality." Persons with this condition are, like all the rest of us, individuals with their own temperament, personality, and ways of handling stress and conflict. However, there is considerable evidence that persons who have cerebral palsy are more *vulnerable* to personality disturbances or emotional conflicts than those who are not so handicapped. Many factors contribute to this vulnerability. If Jennifer's parents find it difficult to accept her and her handicap, they may be unable to provide for her that climate of emotional security which is essential to healthy emotional development. Unless they make special efforts to take her places and do things with her, Jennifer may be so sheltered in the home during her preschool years that she is deprived of needed sensory, intellectual, and social stimulation. The organic damage which her nervous system has sustained may itself have some undesirable effects on her personality and behavior. Because of her disability, Jennifer will be subjected to a larger number of painful and distressing experiences than the average child: hospitalizations, surgical procedures, separation from her parents, and special exercises and appliances which may be inconvenient, embarrassing, and uncomfortable.

Satisfying relationships with other children are also apt to be more difficult for Jennifer than for most children. While still very young she may find herself unwanted as a playmate because she cannot keep up with others. As she grows older, her inability to compete on the playground or in the classroom may deprive her of important opportunities for recognition and status. The time necessary for her to spend in various kinds of therapy may cause her to drop behind her classmates in school. As she grows older, her natural desires to have a career and establish a home of her own may be frustrated by her handicap. In many different ways—some obvious, some quite subtle—Jennifer may be given to understand that she is "different." All of this is apt to have a profound influence on her concept of herself, a damaging effect on her sense of self-worth. It would not be surprising if, faced with continued frustration, Jennifer were often troubled by feelings of inferiority, if she were quite anxious when faced with unfamiliar situations and new experiences, or if she sometimes became introspective and preoccupied with her disability.

To a considerable extent, Jennifer's ability to accept and live creatively with her handicap will depend on the attitude which her parents take toward it and toward her. If they can accept her as she is and give her the love, respect, affection, and security she needs without indulging her or overprotecting her, she will be more likely to accept herself realistically, make the most of her potential and opportunities, and endure and overcome the inevitable frustration which she must encounter. If they are unable to do this, Jennifer may have to carry the burden of an emotional handicap as well as a physical one.

Alike, Yet Very Different

Jennifer, Tammy, and Bret are very different from each other. Jennifer and Tammy are affected by handicaps that can be easily seen by other persons, while Bret looks like a normal child. Both Bret and Jennifer are mentally normal, but have difficulties in communicating with others that will delay their educational development. Tammy is less impaired than they in speech or hearing, yet her ability to communicate is sharply limited by her mental capacity. Bret and Tammy do not suffer from any obvious physical handicap, while Jennifer does have great difficulty in controlling her muscles, limbs, and body movements. The goals, expectations, and roles that each of these children may expect to fulfill in life will be shaped by their respective handicaps in very different ways.

Yet these children do have some things in common. On the one hand, their handicaps differ from other conditions which are equally serious but can often be corrected through proper medical treatment. Many congenital heart defects are limiting and even life-threatening, but respond well to skillful surgical intervention. Cleft lip and palate may seriously affect a child's appearance, feeding habits, and ability to speak, but can usually be corrected or greatly improved through a carefully planned program involving surgery, orthodontia, and speech therapy. On the other hand, the handicaps of Bret, Jennifer, and Tammy also differ from some other conditions which appear in childhood and which are progressive and usually fatal, such as leukemia or cystic fibrosis.

Jennifer, Bret, and Tammy are all affected by conditions that are *irreversible* but *non-progressive*. Nothing can be done to cure or correct the basic injury, defect, or malformation which is responsible for their disability. Each of these children will have to live with some very real limitations, whether physical, mental, perceptual, or social. Yet with the benefit of proper diagnosis and early treatment, with appropriate therapy and education, with sufficient understanding and acceptance, these children may be enabled to adapt to and live with their respective handicaps, and to maximize their very real human potential. Each one is capable of living a significant and valuable life, in spite of his or her disability.

If this is to be accomplished, the persons who will play the key role in the process are not the various professionals who are called upon to diagnose, evaluate, guide, advise, or treat the children, even though their services are absolutely indispensable. The persons who will play the key role in the process are the parents who nurture, supervise, and direct the child's development from day to day. Yet the task of caring for and raising a child with a handicap is a difficult, perplexing, and many-sided responsibility, one for which few if any parents have had any preparation or training. What happens to parents who discover that their child is handicapped, and where they can find help for meeting the demands of this special kind of parenthood?

2

There Must
Be Some
Mistake!

Not Our Child!

Dr. Raymond Remboldt, Director of the Hospital School at
the University of Iowa, is a physician with long experience
in the rehabilitation of handicapped children. Dr. Remboldt
has suggested that the typical response of parents who discover that their child has a serious handicap goes through
three stages.

Their first reaction is likely to be, "No, not us—not our
child! There must be some mistake!" This initial stage is
characterized by shock, denial, and disbelief. In some cases
the parents refuse to accept the physician's diagnosis and take
him from one doctor or clinic to another in the hope of receiving a more favorable evaluation. Some years ago a survey
of mothers of cerebral palsied children revealed that the average family had consulted nine medical doctors, two chiroprac-
tors, and an osteopath in the attempt to secure help for their
child. More recent research, however, suggests this pattern
may have changed. In one recent study, 88 percent of the
families of cerebral palsied children had consulted only two
doctors for a diagnosis.[1]

Even parents who accept their doctor's diagnosis, however,
may find it hard to absorb the impact of this knowledge.

Typical reactions which parents have reported to me are, "It was hard to face the facts," or, "We knew something was wrong, but we didn't want to admit it." One father recalled that he was so distressed he "blacked out" shortly after being told by the doctor that his new-born son would surely suffer from permanent brain damage if he survived.

As we have seen in Chapter 1, some parents arrive at a gradual awareness of their child's handicap by noticing how differently he appears or acts in comparison to other children of his age. Suspecting something is wrong, these parents seek out a physician for confirmation or clarification. Nevertheless, we may surmise that in the early stages of their awareness, they, too, go through a period of not wanting to believe their observations about their child, like the parents who "knew something was wrong but didn't want to admit it."

It is important to recognize that this is not an abnormal or unhealthy reaction on the part of parents. All of us tend to deny, screen out, or discredit information that we find very painful and distressing. These are defensive maneuvers which give our minds time to absorb and to assimilate the significance of knowledge we find difficult to accept. It is only when the initial stage of shock and denial is unduly prolonged that such a reaction becomes unhealthy and immature—that is, when it leads parents to refuse to take their child to a physician for diagnosis and treatment, or when it leads them to take their child from physician to physician in a futile search for a diagnosis that will fit their desires.

Why Our Child?

In the second stage the question changes to "Why *us?* Why was our child born with a handicap when other children are

normal and healthy?" At this point the parents have accepted the *information* that their child is handicapped but their
feelings are still in rebellion against that reality. They are
experiencing the pain of deep disappointment, which may be
expressed in *anger, guilt,* or *grief.*

Anger may arise out of the need for someone to "blame"
for the tragedy the parents are experiencing, to locate someone who is at fault. It may be directed against the physician
who delivered the child for supposed negligence, even though
this is infrequently a factor. It may be directed against a
spouse or a spouse's family, who are thought to be responsible for some hereditary defect. It may be directed against
the parent himself for either real or imagined actions which
he feels have contributed to the child's disability. One mother
whose cerebral palsied child had been born out of wedlock
had attempted to produce an abortion during her pregnancy.
When the child's handicap was later discovered, she felt responsible, until her physician reassured her that it was unlikely she had caused her child's handicap. Anger and resentment may also be directed at God, who is regarded as being
in either direct or at least ultimate control of all events and
circumstances, and therefore responsible for the child's handicap. A mother who had a fifteen-year-old mentally retarded
son and a second child with cerebral palsy described her reaction in the following way: "God had been very cruel. I
thought, 'Why did he give me two, instead of one healthy
child?' " A mother whose small daughter was very severely
handicapped recalled her early resentment, and its resolution.

> I couldn't see why they [*sic*] had chosen her to be
> this way. It made me awfully sour against the church
> and God. I gave up and wouldn't go to church. But
> after our minister and different ones in the church
> came out, I could see I wasn't doing myself any good

by trying to spite God and the church. So I've gone back to church, and I've started teaching Sunday school, which I think has helped a lot. I can see now that it was foolish to blame anyone, but I was so upset I had to blame someone, and I didn't know who to blame.

Two things are suggested by this mother's statement: "I was so upset I had to blame someone." For one thing, her anger and resentment were a reaction to the severe emotional wound which she had sustained when her child was found to have cerebral palsy, an attempt to defend herself against the pain of that experience. These feelings had to find some outlet. But we also notice this anger was not an enduring state of mind; the concern and understanding her pastor and fellow church members were able to communicate to her and the support they were able to give her in this crisis enabled her to move beyond resentment to renewed trust.

Guilt is frequently experienced by parents whose child is handicapped. Out of twenty-two families of cerebral palsied children whom I have interviewed, nine indicated that they had felt at some time or other they were to blame for their child's handicap. Only three, however—all mothers—still felt this way at the time they were interviewed. One believed that she had continued to work too long into her pregnancy; another believed her child's handicap was caused by her failure to call a physician quickly enough when the child was ill with a high fever at age three months. The third said, simply and sadly, "Since I was the one carrying him, I feel like I was responsible." It is evident that the guilt which some parents feel over their child's handicap need not have any basis in fact. Often it has none, and the parents' physician will probably try to counter such feeling of guilt. Over half the families in the author's study reported that they had never felt at fault for their child's condition.

A number of writers have suggested that the response of parents to the birth of a handicapped child can best be understood as a form of *grief*.[2] According to this view, the psychological preparation for birth during pregnancy involves both the wish for a perfect child and the fear of a damaged child. Even when the newborn child is normal and healthy, there is apt to be some discrepancy between the parents' expectations and reality. However, when the child is born with a defect or handicap, the parents are faced with the sudden "loss" of the wished-for, expected baby, and are confronted instead with a child who evokes fear and anger. They adapt to this experience through a process of *mourning*: their longings for a "perfect" child are recalled, felt intensely, and then gradually relinquished, thus liberating their interests and feelings for a realistic relationship with their *actual* child.

However, this process is made difficult by two factors. First, it takes place at a time when the mother is depleted both physically and emotionally from labor and delivery. Second, while the parents are working through their grief for the hoped-for child they have lost, they must also learn to respond to the needs of their actual, handicapped child, whom they may see as having caused the "death" of the child they had hoped for.

There are two ways in which parents may meet this crisis unsuccessfully.

On the one hand, the injury to their self-esteem may be so painful that it causes them to reject the child outright and to deny their relationship to it. A recent educational film records the actual story of a baby born in Washington, D.C., with two congenital defects, Down's syndrome (mongolism) and the absence of any opening between the stomach and the small intestine. The latter defect could have been corrected without great difficulty by means of a well-known surgical procedure. However, the parents were so overwhelmed with disappointment that their child was mongoloid that they refused to permit the necessary operation. As a result, the child died in the hospital about two weeks after birth from lack of nourishment. This is of course an extreme instance. Such open rejection of a handicapped child is seldom seen. Yet there are some parents who struggle inwardly for years with feelings of disappointment and rejection toward their handicapped child.

In order to explore such feelings, I asked parents of children with cerebral palsy to respond to the following statement:

> Some parents of handicapped children have said there were times when they wondered whether it might have been better if their child had not lived. How do you feel about that?

Many vigorously denied the suggestion that they had wished for their child's death. Although only a few families could give even tentative acceptance to this attitude, several reported they had held such feelings at one time. One family wondered why a neighbor's daughter who was healthy and normal had been killed in an accident, while their son was born handicapped. "Everybody has to die sometime. Why not J. instead of her? But you just can't think like that." The mother of a twelve-year-old, severely handicapped boy said that she had "often wished they had never saved him. What did they save him for? He's a physical wreck. Yet he is such a lovely child. He's such a nice little boy." The mother of a fourteen-year-old boy, only slightly less handicapped than the previous child, said, "If he had been born dead, yes. But as far as wishing he had died—that's like asking me to kill him! Nobody would ever dare try to take him away from me." It was

evident that these parents did have feelings of rejection toward
their children, but it was equally clear that they were uncomfortable with these feelings, that they were conflicted
about them and struggled against them. They could not affirm the desire for their child's death without immediately
denying it: "You just can't think like that," or, "He's such
a nice little boy."

On the other hand, some parents react not by openly rejecting their child, but by burying their anger and covering
it up with over-attachment and devotion to the child. A number of studies have indicated that parents of handicapped
children are likely to be overly protective toward their children. In one survey of the life history of cerebral palsied persons the researchers reported that 30 of the 63 persons studied were either moderately or severely disturbed emotionally,
and 27 had been so overprotected by their parents that they
were described as "infantilized." [3] It is generally agreed that
such a reaction is harmful to the child, for it may result in
his being excused from treatment or therapy which is essential but painful or unpleasant, or in being so sheltered at home
that he is deprived of needed stimulation during the preschool
years, or in being prevented from achieving a sense of self-
worth and independence from his parents. It seems clear that
parents who are overprotective are responding primarily to
their *own* needs—handling their feelings of guilt, resentment,
and rejection—rather than to the needs of their child.

The mourning process may thus be much more difficult
for parents whose child is born disabled than for those whose
child has actually died. Both must deal with painful feelings
of loss, disappointment, intense longings, resentment, and
guilt. But for the parents of the handicapped child, especially
for the mother, the daily and unremitting demands of the
child for care and attention mean that their emotional invest-
ment cannot simply be withdrawn as when a child dies. Thus

for some parents, the grief which they experience over the birth of their disabled child may not be an acutely painful but transitory episode, but rather may become a permanently fixed attitude toward life which one author has described as "chronic sorrow."

One mother reported her initial feelings about her son's cerebral palsy in language that conveys a vivid sense of grief and mourning:

> Any woman who is going to have a baby dreams—not of a future president—but of the cub scout, the Little Leaguer, raiding the cookie jar, first dates. . . . But the minute you say, "cerebral palsy," that child is gone forever. It's just like that child has been killed. Here you have another child—you love it just as much—but it's not the one you dreamed of. It ends everything for that one child you've dreamed of. What you can make of the cerebral palsied child is something quite different.

What Can We Do to Help?

The third stage in parents' response to a child's handicap comes when they ask, "What can we do about it?" When the shock and denial have passed and their anger, guilt, and grief have been largely worked through, parents are able to turn from their own needs to the needs of their child and ask, "What can we do to help this child develop to his maximum capacities?" At this point they are beginning to accept both the child *and* his handicap. They are overcoming a futile preoccupation with what might have been, and are coming to terms with the reality of what is. They are beginning to turn their thoughts from the past to the present and the future, and to reach out for appropriate help.

Of course this does not happen in clearly-defined stages. Some parents struggle inwardly with feelings of resentment or guilt for months or even years after they have taken steps to secure care and treatment for their child. Others begin to reach out for help very early, even before they can quite believe something is seriously wrong with their child, by taking him to a physician or clinic for an examination. Yet there does seem to be a kind of natural progression in these three stages; and the final stage marks the beginning of positive action on the child's behalf.

We cannot emphasize too strongly how necessary it is for parents to work through this process to completion: to move from initial shock and denial through the painful sense of loss and disappointment to the point where they are able realistically to accept the child *and* his handicap, and to love, respect, and enjoy him *with* all his limitations, in relative freedom from resentment, shame, and guilt. It is necessary not simply for the parents' emotional health and well-being, but even more necessary for the sake of the child himself.

Almost all workers with handicapped children regard the attitudes of parents as playing an absolutely crucial role in the child's development. It is in relationship to his parents that a child first becomes aware of himself as an individual person. His own picture of himself is formed largely out of the images which they reflect back to him; they are like a mirror from which he derives his sense of his own worth and value, his own unique "shape" as a person. It is inevitable that their feelings and attitudes toward his handicap will be incorporated in his own attitudes toward himself. If his parents regard his handicap as a painful and unpleasant burden given them to bear, the child himself may come to feel like a burden to his parents. If they are ashamed of his disability, the child may harbor a deep sense of shame about himself. If they see his disability as a form of divine punishment, the child may feel rejected and "cursed" for reasons he cannot understand. However, when parents can accept their handicapped child as a person worthy of respect and love, with God-given potential to be developed, then the child can learn to respect himself with his abilities and limitations, and to regard his disability not as a curse but as a challenge.

This may seem to place a heavy burden of responsibility on parents, and indeed it does. Yet few parents of handicapped children would say that the burden is an impossible one. In one experiment more than 2000 persons were asked to rank ten handicapping conditions according to their estimate of the seriousness of each. Among the conditions to be ranked were cerebral palsy, mental retardation, brain injury, blindness, and deafness; and among the persons surveyed were parents whose children suffered from these five handicaps. *None of those who were parents of handicapped youngsters ranked their own child's handicap as the most serious.*[4] It appears that persons who live intimately with a particular handicap see it differently than those who view it from a distance; they do not regard it as so threatening; they can accept it more easily than those who do not know it first-hand.

Nearly two-thirds of the parents in my own study reported that they found it easier to accept their child's cerebral palsy at the time of the interview than when they had first discovered it. Only two of the twenty-two families said it had become more difficult for them to live with the situation as time passed. Further, when asked if they had experienced any rewards in having a child who was handicapped, all but two families said they had. Among the benefits they mentioned were their satisfaction in the child's accomplishments, the feeling that they had been singled out for a special task, their sense of closeness to the child because of his disability, the belief that their handicapped child was unusually responsive and affectionate, and the feeling that they had become more understanding of other people as a result of this experience.

It was clear that none of these parents viewed their child's disability as an unrelieved tragedy. Although it had been and in some cases remained painful and distressing for them, most of them were making a successful effort to view their child's handicap in as favorable a light as possible, and to find meaning and satisfaction *in* the experience, not simply *in spite of* it. For a number of the parents, religious faith was one of the factors which supported and strengthened this attitude. Let us turn our attention, then, to the role which religion may play in this experience.

3

Finding Help
Through
Your Faith

Three Different Viewpoints

Bret's parents do not consider themselves religious people. They neither participate in nor belong to a church or synagogue. Their lives revolve around Mr. Holloway's work, their home and family, their friends, and various community responsibilities. To them, Bret's handicap has no particular religious significance; it is simply an unfortunate accident of birth, a circumstance which he and they must learn to live with as best they can. Although they were deeply distressed when they discovered Bret was deaf, it was in no way for them a crisis of faith or values or of the meaning of their life. If someone were to ask them *why* Bret was born without hearing, they would probably answer, "It just happened, that's all. Every so often a child is born deaf, and Bret happens to be one of those children."

Tammy's parents have perceived her handicap in a rather different way. They are dutiful, if somewhat conventional, churchgoers who believe that whatever happens, happens because God has willed it. In the beginning they had feelings of anger and resentment, both toward God and toward their fellow church members. They felt as though God had let them down, as though he had been unfair to them. "Why did he do this?" they asked. "We've tried to do right, to be good Christians, responsible parents. Why do so many people who don't want children or don't care for them properly have healthy youngsters, while our Tammy is retarded?" They wondered if they were being punished for some failure or mistake. Their first child had arrived only seven months after their wedding. Were they—and Tammy—now having to "pay" for that indiscretion? It seemed to them that others in their church were "looking down" on them for having become parents of a mongoloid child, and for a long time it was hard to take Tammy with them to church because they felt people were staring at them with pity or curiosity. But the Nelsons have talked with their pastor about many of these feelings, and have come to feel differently about Tammy's handicap. They still think of her mongolism as in some sense "God's will," but they no longer regard it as *punishment*. "Whatever God does, he does for some good reason," they now say. "We don't know what reason he had in giving us a retarded child, but we believe he has a reason for it, and that he intends something good out of it. Being responsible for Tammy is a kind of special 'calling' God has given us." They believe not only that God chose them for this especially demanding kind of parenthood, but that having done so he will also guide and support them and help them fulfill their "calling."

Jennifer's parents are also religious people. They attend church services fairly regularly. Before Jennifer was born they were adult counselors for a youth group in the church. They enjoy a close relationship with their pastor. But they vigorously reject the idea that God might have caused Jennifer to be born with cerebral palsy. If someone asks them why she is handicapped, they are likely to mention medical factors which might have caused her brain damage. They do not think of God as *directly* responsible for all events. To them, God is always on the side of health and healing. Although they see Jennifer's handicap as a tragic accident, they do believe that God is working through their physicians, therapists, social worker, pastor, and others to help Jennifer achieve the fullest life possible for her. "Some day, with God's help, doctors will learn how to prevent handicaps like cerebral palsy," they say. Unlike the Nelsons, they are reluctant to think of themselves as especially chosen to be the parents of a handicapped child ("That sounds so righteous!"), yet they do believe that God is working with and through them to help Jennifer realize her full potential as a person.

From these brief descriptions we can see how religion may influence a family's response to their child's handicap in a number of different ways. It may be a very important factor in shaping their response, or it may be insignificant. It may help them view their situation positively with acceptance, hope, and confidence; or it may contribute to the pain, distress, and perplexity of their situation. The precise role that religion plays for any family in such a crisis will depend on many other factors, including the temperament, character, and personality of the parents; their previous religious training and belief; and the extent of their involvement with and participation in their church or synagogue. We cannot, however, predict how parents will respond to this crisis simply by knowing whether they are Catholic, Protestant, Jewish, or unchurched, or by knowing whether they attend worship weekly, monthly, or only twice a year. Religion is too intimate, personal, and complex a thing for that. The eminent psychologist, Gordon Allport, observed that each person's religious faith is in some sense uniquely his own and different from that of any other individual.

One of the factors that may affect parents' response to a child's handicap is the way in which they view the *meaning of suffering*. They may perceive the handicap in very different ways (as a curse or a blessing, as punishment or a special calling, as an accident or something that was "meant to be"), according to the way they understand the meaning of suffering. The meaning of suffering is a central theme in the teachings of most religious traditions. Yet, the person who asks, "Why did this illness happen to me (or to my loved one)?" will seldom find his church or his faith presenting him with a single, clear-cut answer. Even within the same religious tradition, a bewildering variety of possible answers may be suggested to his question.

One writer found five different answers to the question, "Why did this handicap happen?" among the members of a single congregation.[5] Some believed that God had sent the handicap as a form of punishment, either for the sins of the disabled person or for the sins of some member of his family. Others saw the handicap as a "cross" which God had given the person to bear as a sign of his love. Still other persons believed that the purpose of the handicap was to help the individual discover and make known God's strength through his own weakness. There were also those who, although they did not understand *why* the handicap had happened, nevertheless believed that "all things work together for good to those who love God." Finally, there were some persons who maintained that God had nothing to do with the handicap; but that with increased scientific and medical understanding men will someday be able to correct or prevent handicaps. Each of these answers could be supported by references to the Bible or to subsequent religious literature, past or present.

Some Questions—and Some Answers

One reason the meaning of suffering is so complex an issue is that it really contains at least three questions for the religious person.

1. Is God the author or *source* of the affliction? If so, in what sense or to what extent is he responsible for it?

2. What is the *value* of this experience to the person or persons involved? Is it totally harmful, or may the sufferer benefit from it in some way or other?

3. What *attitude* should one adopt toward this experience?

The problem can be represented by a simple diagram, consisting of two axes, one horizonal, the other vertical, as shown in *Figure 1*.

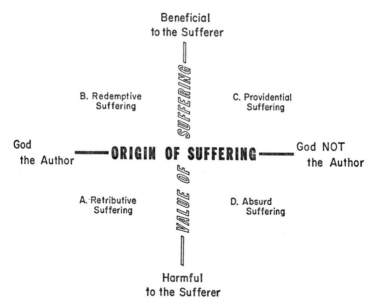

Figure 1. The Meanings of Suffering:
a Conceptual Framework

The horizontal line represents possible answers to the question, "Does this suffering come from God?" At the left end of the line are those answers which assume that God sends the affliction, whether as a punishment for sin, to strengthen the sufferer's character, or to provide a way of salvation. At the right end of the line are those answers which trace the origin of suffering to forces opposed to God, such as the demons or evil spirits mentioned in the New Testament. In between these two poles we may locate those answers which attribute suffering to natural causes or human freedom. Here God is understood as *permitting* suffering, even though he may not directly cause or intend it for the individual.

The vertical line represents answers to the question, "Is there any good to be derived from this experience?" At the bottom of the line we place those views which see illness, disability, and pain as serving no good purpose whatever to the afflicted person, as wholly detrimental to his well-being. The top end of the line represents those answers which stress the benefits of suffering, whether as a form of discipline, a test of character, a way of atoning for sins, a witness to God's grace, or a means of communion with God. Suffering understood as punishment could be located either on the upper or the lower half of the vertical line, depending on the way punishment is viewed. If its purpose is simply retribution, then it must be harmful to the person being punished. If, however, punishment is intended to reform or rehabilitate the sufferer, it must in the long run be beneficial, and belongs on the upper half of the line.

So we can see four major ways in which suffering might be interpreted religiously, each one corresponding to a different section of the diagram.

In the lower left quarter God is seen as the source of the affliction, and the experience is viewed as harmful to the person. Suffering must then be understood as an expression of God's wrath or judgment, that is to say, as a form of *punish-*

ment. That sickness or misfortune have often been interpreted in this light can be seen from many passages in both the Old and New Testaments. Miriam is struck with leprosy for opposing Moses' marriage to an Egyptian woman (Num. 12:1-15) ; the child born to the illicit union of David and Bathsheba dies (2 Sam. 12:16-23) ; King Uzziah is afflicted with leprosy because he took to himself the priestly privilege of burning incense on the altar of Yahweh (2 Chron. 26:16-21) ; Ananias and Sapphira fall dead when their attempt to defraud the church is exposed (Acts 5:1-11) ; and Paul tells the congregation at Corinth that the reason some of them have become ill and others have died is that they have profaned the Lord's Supper (1 Cor. 11:27-30). Behind this conception of suffering as a consequence of sin lies the belief that *all* things—poverty and prosperity, illness and health, life and death—come from God.

On at least one occasion, however, Jesus flatly rejected the notion that all suffering can be understood as punishment. Confronted by a blind man, he is asked, "Rabbi, who sinned, this man or his parents, that he is born blind?" Jesus replies, "It was not that this man sinned, or his parents, but that the works of God might be made manifest in him" (John 9:1-7). He shifts attention from the *cause* of the affliction to its *purpose;* and though he does not deny that the man's blindness may serve a divine purpose, he does deny that it is intended as a form of *punishment.*

The upper left quarter of the diagram shows God as the source of the suffering, but views it as a benefit or blessing, an expression not of God's anger but of his love. Suffering is thus a part of the process of *redemption.* It may be regarded as a painful but necessary form of discipline (Prov. 3:11-12), as a form of witness or testimony which the suffering person is privileged to hear on behalf of God (2 Cor. 12:7-9), or as a way of sharing in the suffering and victory of Christ and thus entering into the most intimate kind of fellowship with him (Phil. 3:7-11). Whatever its specific purpose, suffering is seen as a sign of God's gracious care and concern, a divine gift that may be accepted with joy and thanksgiving.

> We rejoice in our sufferings, knowing that suffering produces endurance, and endurance produces character, and character produces hope, and hope does not disappoint us, because God's love has been poured into our hearts through the Holy Spirit which has been given to us (Rom. 5:3-5).

The upper right section of the diagram does not represent God as the direct cause of the affliction. Nevertheless it views it as potentially beneficial to the sufferer. Interpretations such as this stress that suffering is only a temporary state of affairs for the person of faith, and that even here and now God is able to transform the evil of pain and loss into good for the afflicted person.

> I consider that the sufferings of this present time are not worth comparing with the glory that is to be revealed to us. . . . For we know that in everything God works for good with those who love him, who are called according to his purpose (Rom. 8:18, 28).

Such views may be called *providential.*

Finally, *the lower right section* of the diagram shows illness and suffering as harmful, and as having their origin in nature, human error, or in demonic forces. Persons who view suffering in this way are apt to regard it as meaningless or *absurd,* like the late French writer Albert Camus. With Job, they may cry,

> Behold, I go forward, but he is not there;
> and backward, but I cannot perceive him;

on the left hand I seek him, but I cannot behold him;
I turn to the right hand, but I cannot see him.

(Job 23:8-9)

Although at first glance this may not seem to be a very "religious" approach to illness, it seems to be strikingly similar to Jesus' attitude toward pain and disease. As we read the narratives of Jesus' healing ministry in the first three Gospels, we do not discover any suggestion that God is the source of disease or that sickness is of any benefit to the sufferer. The only value attached to illness is the opportunity it provides for showing the nearness of God's kingdom. In the power of this kingdom, Jesus strives mightily to resist and overcome pain, disease, and evil. The only good thing he finds in sickness lies in getting rid of it. This attitude is quite close to the understanding of suffering as *absurd*.

Now we can see the answers that may be given to the last question, "What is the appropriate attitude toward this experience of pain or loss?" For the person who understands his suffering as punishment, the proper attitude would seem to be *penitent submission* to God's judgment. The person who is convinced that God intends his illness or disability for his own good will understand it as *redemptive,* and will respond more appropriately with attitudes of *acceptance, cooperation,* and perhaps even *gratitude.* On the other hand, the person who believes that God did not send or intend his suffering but can nevertheless turn it to his ultimate good, will meet his experience with attitudes of *faith, patience,* and *hope,* trusting in God's providence. Finally, the person who sees suffering as essentially *absurd* will most likely respond either with determined *resistance* in the attempt to overcome his affliction, or, if this is impossible, with courageous *endurance.* These possibilities are diagrammed in Figure 2.

B. Redemptive Suffering:	C. Providential Suffering:
acceptance, cooperation gratitude	faith, patience, hope
A. Retributive Suffering	D. Absurd Suffering
patient submission	determined resistance, courageous endurance,

Figure 2.   Attitudes Toward Suffering

Now we can better understand the responses of the three families described at the beginning of this chapter. The Holloways view Bret's deafness as largely meaningless or *absurd;* their efforts are devoted to helping him overcome a disability in which they see no purpose or value. Tammy's parents have moved from an initial perception of her mongolism as *punishment* to a viewpoint that may be regarded as *redemptive:* they believe God sent this handicap for some hidden but benevolent purpose. Jennifer's parents view her cerebral palsy in a largely *providential* context: they see God working in and with them to help realize some good out of what at first was a very painful loss.

Two words of caution should be added before going any further. First, these alternatives are not mutually exclusive or incompatible, except as they apply to a particular experience of illness or disability. It is not illogical to suppose that different kinds of suffering could be found to fit each of these four interpretations. Surely human pain comes in too many forms and shapes to be understood in one way only.

Second, the outline presented above is simply a framework for understanding, and nothing more. It may provide some order for what is otherwise a bewildering variety of possibilities. Living persons—especially those passing through a crisis in their lives—cannot neatly be herded into one section or another of a diagram. It is not surprising to find a person swinging back and forth between several points of view as he tries to make sense out of his own suffering. He may even hold what seems to be contradictory attitudes at one and the same time, like one mother who expressed the belief that her child's disability was "just a statistical probability," yet that it was also "meant to be."

What Parents Believe

Now that we have seen the variety of possibilities available for understanding the meaning of a handicap or disability in religious terms, what can we say about the way in which families with handicapped children actually view their own situation?

Early research in the field of rehabilitation often emphasized the tendency of parents to regard their child's handicap as *punishment*. In one such study involving mothers of cerebral palsied children, 62 percent answered "yes" to the question, "Do you feel your child is handicapped as punishment to you?" [6]

More recent research, however, suggests that this attitude has changed. In my own study, every parent but one vigorously rejected the suggestion that their child's cerebral palsy might be a form of divine punishment. Only one mother agreed hesitantly that "it might be," but then went on to say that if it were, "you're not going to know because God has already willed it before it happens." Further, even if the child's handicap were punishment, she insisted, "There's good that will come out of it."

The only unqualified acceptance of the punishment theme came from a mother whose very severely handicapped son was 15 and thus too old to permit her to be included in the research group. Her reaction is so unusual that it is worth reporting, however. She told how she had lost faith in God as a result of her child's handicap, and had subsequently regained it, but in a different form.

> As a child I used to be real religious—I read the Bible a lot. When this happened, I thought, "What have I done that was so bad that God would let this innocent child be born a cripple?" Then I thought, "There can't be a God who would be so mean as to let this happen to so many people." Then not so long ago I read some books about Edgar Cayce, and got on this reincarnation bit. This is the only thing that makes sense to me. The only way I could feel there was any reason for Andy to have cerebral palsy was the law of karma: he had been bad in some other life and this was his punishment. And then this would explain why I have diabetes and am saddled with Andy's care. This is the only way I can believe in God. If God were good, he wouldn't let Andy be handicapped for no reason.

This mother had not attended church since her childhood; moreover, there was no one else—not even her husband— with whom she could discuss her newfound belief. Her religion was a very private and personal part of her life, yet it was extremely important to her. Her statement indicates that even though she could interpret suffering only in retributive terms, yet it was necessary for her to find some acceptable religious meaning in this painful experience.

There is additional evidence that the parents interviewed

by the author strongly rejected both the *punishment* and *absurd* perspectives on suffering. Each was given a set of 34 statements expressing a wide variety of beliefs and attitudes toward suffering and illness. The statements were printed on individual cards, and the respondents were asked to sort them into five groups: one statement with which they agreed, and another with which they disagreed most strongly; eight additional statements each with which they agreed and disagreed, but less strongly; and a remaining group of sixteen statements about which they felt least agreement or disagreement. The two statements with which parents most frequently expressed strong disagreement were, "Suffering comes to us as God's punishment for our sins," and, "The existence of pain and disease shows that the world cannot be the creation of a loving God." The former statement is a clear expression of the punishment view of suffering, and the latter may be seen as an expression of the view that suffering is absurd. Only one parent out of the entire 36 gave strong agreement to a statement expressing the latter perspective: "It's hard to understand how a loving God can allow pain and disease to exist in the world."

The statements most strongly affirmed by the parents were:

> God has a purpose for every person's life, even though we may find it hard to understand that purpose.
>
> Whatever may befall us, God is always near to help and strengthen us.
>
> All things work together for good to those who love God.

All of these are optimistic, future-directed, and tend to evoke attitudes of faith, patience, and hope, and can be regarded as falling within that perspective which has been called *providential*.

One statement drew both strong agreement and disagreement from parents: "Whatever happens, happens as a result of the will of God." It is an ambiguous statement, but a powerful one. To some parents it seemed to suggest the *punishment* view of their child's handicap, hence they rejected it. To others it appeared to carry a different meaning. During the interviews, nearly two-thirds of the parents said they believed that in some way their child's handicap was "the will of God." About half of these went on to explain, "There's a purpose in everything." We may surmise that parents who agreed strongly with the statement quoted above did so because to them it suggested purpose and hope in the difficult circumstances through which they were living.

It appears, then, that most parents of handicapped children reject views of suffering as *meaningless* or as a form of *punishment,* and affirm views which see it as *redemptive* or *providential*—that is, as carrying within it seeds of purpose, meaning, hope, and the possibility of some larger and more inclusive benefit.

Religion: Liability or Asset?

Do the families of children who are handicapped find religion to be a liability or an asset? In one survey, 84 percent of the parents reported that they had found religion helpful in adjusting to the problem of their child's handicap, and an even slightly higher percent said they found prayer helpful.[7] Since this researcher did not inquire whether religion might have actually made the parents' adjustment more *difficult,* I asked parents whether religion had been a help or a hindrance to them, or neither. A smaller proportion had found religion helpful (73 percent), but no parent answered that it had been a hindrance in coping with the problems of his child's handicap. Those who did not feel religion had helped them regarded it as a neutral factor, and it is of interest that two-thirds of this group attended religious services either very irregularly or not at all.

Nevertheless, there were some cases in which it appeared that religion had contributed to the distress of the parents. More than a third of the families had experienced some religious questions, doubts, or conflicts related to their child's handicap, although most of them had been resolved before the study took place. As might be expected the most common question was, "Why did this happen to us?" or "Why did it happen to our child?" Although this appeared to have been a major, continuing issue for only two families, the theme recurred with enough frequency and strength that it could not be ignored. The handicap was experienced as a challenge or even a threat to the faith, beliefs, and values of some parents. "If God is good, and God is almighty, why does he allow children to be born disabled?" "What have we done—what can this child have done—to deserve such punishment?"

There is some reason to believe that this question may be more troublesome to people who are actively religious than those who are not. It may well be, as C. S. Lewis has suggested, that suffering is more of a problem for religious people than for non-religious, because they have come to expect more of God. Perhaps for some persons, religious belief adds to the experience of suffering what has been called "cognitive dissonance." One aspect of the believer's experience—i.e., the birth of a handicapped child—is jarringly out-of-tune with another—his faith in an all-powerful and all-loving God. This out-of-tuneness sets up a state of tension or inner conflict which demands to be reduced. Thus for some persons religion may actually heighten the stress which they experience by adding to it the additional question of the *meaning* of the affliction.

Also, it may be that some persons who are outwardly "religious" really expect that somehow they will be rewarded for their piety by being protected from pain and loss. Although such a view is repudiated by numerous passages in both the Old and New Testaments as well as by most contemporary religious writers on suffering, it no doubt continues to exist at some level in the minds of even devout and intelligent church members.

Besides introducing questions, doubts, and conflicts over the meaning of the handicap, religion could be seen contributing to the pain some families felt in yet another way. A number of the parents whom I interviewed were "turned off" by what they perceived as the curiosity or pity persons in their church showed toward their handicapped child. One family reported that they attended church infrequently since the birth of their handicapped child because they felt people in their church were staring at them and talking about them. Another parent did not want the persons in her church to assist her in caring for her child because that would mean they were "feeling sorry" for her. To be sure, these attitudes may be incorrectly perceived by the parents. Even if their perceptions are accurate, the curiosity and pity they resent are not directly related to religious beliefs or teachings. Yet if the minister and congregation are not able to communicate genuine interest and concern for the family and their child *along with* a sense of deep respect, this feeling of being stigmatized and alienated from the religious community must be recognized as a factor contributing to the parents' distress.

However, none of the families studied by the author found religion a major obstacle in dealing with the problems of their child's handicap. On the whole, they saw it as either neutral or positively helpful. In no instance was a parent found using religious ideas or practices in order to deny the reality of a handicap, or to escape the necessity of accepting and dealing with it. None of the parents seemed to be living in the hope of a magical or miraculous "cure," whether by religious or medical means.

In what way did the families find religion helpful? Some stated that they "couldn't have got along without religion"; others felt it had helped them "accept" the handicap. Still others responded that religion "makes you feel better," or that it "gives consolation," "peace of mind," "inner strength," or "helps you understand." Since these helps, though significant to the parents, are somewhat general, let us examine the specific ways in which religion helped parents adapt to their child's handicap.

1. For some families, religion seemed to reinforce the reality of their loss, and help them to "face the facts," however painful and disturbing these facts were. One implication of the belief that the child's handicap is "the will of God" seems to be that what is God's will is inevitable and unalterable. It cannot be avoided or denied; it must be accepted; that is, the parents must resign themselves to the fact that this child is *not* the child they had hoped for, nor will he ever become that child. He has some real and inescapable limitations which they must recognize, and with which both he and they will have to live.

2. Religion also appeared to soften the apparent harshness of the child's disability. It enabled parents to see elements of both purpose and hope in their situation. As already noted, half of the parents who accepted their child's handicap as the will of God went on to say, in one way or another, "There's a purpose in everything that happens." The view of suffering that received the strongest agreement from the

group expressed this same thought: because God intends our ultimate good in everything he allows to happen, no event, however painful or distressing, can be seen as an unrelieved tragedy. The fact that very few of the parents had found no reward at all in having a child who was handicapped, and that nearly all of them strongly rejected the idea that it might have been better had their child died, is consistent with this attitude. On the human level, the consequence of believing in a divine purpose is *hope:* if God has a purpose for every person's life, and if every event in life has some meaningful part to play in that purpose, then we can face the future with confidence. In this connection, we remember that the statements about suffering most frequently affirmed were future-oriented and optimistic. Also, one of the reasons parents believed their child's handicap had become easier to accept as time passed was that they had learned how much could be done to help the child. This represents the reinforcement of hope in a tangible, concrete way.

3. Religion seemed to help in a third way: by providing motivation, direction, and support for the ongoing task of parenthood. As one mother put it, "I think that if I hadn't had the faith I have, I wouldn't have been able to take on the job I have." Half of the families who had an active church relationship felt that in some way their handicapped child was a special calling or vocation given them by God. One mother put it in these words:

> This is the way I feel: we in the Catholic church always feel you have a "calling" for this or that. I was always an honor student, a leader. In my nurse's training, the people in charge would always say, "You must be chosen for something very special," because I had these qualities. I would always think, "I don't really feel called, I don't feel that

special." When this happened, I thought maybe I was really being prepared for this unknowingly, this must be what I was being prepared for.

Although religion may occasionally add to the distress of having a child who is handicapped, for many families it becomes a very significant resource for dealing creatively and constructively with their situation.

4

What Can
We Do?

We have seen that the last stage in
parents' response to their child's
handicap begins when they ask, "What can we do to help?"
In this chapter we want to look in some detail at the process
by which parents reach out for assistance so that their child
develops his full potential as a person.

What the Child Needs

In order to seek appropriate help for their child, it is first of
all necessary for parents to understand the handicapped child's
basic needs. Many of these he shares with all children, normal as well as handicapped. However, the child who is handicapped may need special help in satisfying some of these
needs; and sometimes the needs themselves are expressed in
ways that are different than for the non-handicapped child.

All children, of course, have certain inescapable *physical*
needs: to be fed, clothed, sheltered, to be cared for when sick
or injured. The human infant comes into the world the most
helpless of all creatures, unable to do anything for himself
but breathe, eat, sleep, eliminate waste from his body, and
cry when he is hungry or uncomfortable. He is totally dependent on his parents for nurture and protection, and he remains

dependent on them for a much longer period than the young of any other species.

This is true of the normal, healthy infant, but it is even more true of the child with a handicap. His physical needs may be more difficult to satisfy, or may impose unusual demands on his parents. If he is neurologically handicapped, he may have difficulty taking nourishment. Some handicaps seem to make the child unusually vulnerable to certain illnesses (for example, mongoloid children tend to have more than their share of respiratory disorders). Further, the child with a handicap may be physically dependent on his parents for a much longer time than the normal baby. A father may carry his year-old daughter in his arms with pride and pleasure; but if she is nine years old and unable to walk because of spine bifida or cerebral palsy, carrying her from the house to the car and from the car to her school classroom may become wearisome.

Every child also has certain *emotional* needs which are just as essential in their own way as the physical needs just mentioned. All children need the security and trust that come from receiving warmth and affection, and from the realization that their parents love them and care deeply and dependably for them. They experience this in part as their physical needs are met: they are fed when hungry, changed when wet or soiled, cuddled when frightened or lonely. They also receive this when mother or father respond to their smiles and coos, and when they show pride in the child's accomplishments, even though for the child who is disabled some of these may be quite limited or long delayed.

Children also need to have limits set for their behavior until they are mature enough to begin to set limits for themselves. Some of these limits are for the child's protection: the stove is hot and must not be touched; the street is dangerous and he may go there only with mother or father. Other limits however concern the needs and wishes of other persons; the growing child has to learn to wait for attention when mother is busy, to share toys and take turns with brothers and sisters, to accept "no" without a temper tantrum. Some parents find it hard to say "no" to their handicapped child. It seems as though life itself has placed so many limits on him that they are reluctant to add any more to the list. But this attitude may not serve the best interests of their child. Even though the child with a handicap experiences more than his share of life's inevitable frustrations, it is still necessary for parents to set limits to his behavior, to provide kindly but consistent discipline. The parents who feel so "sorry" for their child that they find it impossible to say "no" to him will overindulge him, and will fail to help meet one of his most basic emotional needs.

Like all children, the child with a handicap also needs to develop a growing sense of independence from his parents. All of us have seen the small child who stubbornly refuses to allow mother to feed him or help him dress: "I do it myself!" Even though it would be faster or neater for mother to continue to do these things for the child, she knows how important it is for him to master these tasks himself, how much his own sense of worth is enhanced by learning to depend on himself. The child who is handicapped may have a great deal more difficulty mastering those skills which confer independence than the normal child, and his accomplishments may be much longer in coming. Indeed, some children are so handicapped that they will never become fully independent, either economically or physically. Yet every child needs the opportunity to achieve the fullest measure of independence possible for him, and to be encouraged to do as much as possible for himself. It will be difficult at times for the parents of the handicapped child to permit him to feed or dress himself when he does it so slowly or so untidily, or to let him walk with so much effort from the house to the car when they could carry him so easily. But parents who recognize how basic is their child's need to become independent will restrain themselves in order to allow the child to do as much as he can for himself.

All children need to develop a feeling of self-acceptance and respect. Much of this comes naturally as other emotional needs are being met—when they experience warmth and affection, when appropriate limits are set, when they are encouraged in their efforts to be independent. The handicapped child, however, may have to struggle to achieve this goal. He must learn first of all to accept his handicap, to recognize that it does make him somewhat different from other children, to understand it insofar as possible, and to talk about it with other people free of shame or embarrassment. If his parents can talk about it with him in a matter-of-fact way and answer his questions about it as they arise in words he can understand, he will learn to do this much more easily. If they cannot speak of it, or if they can refer to it only with shame or pity, the child himself will have a difficult time learning to talk about it easily and naturally.

The handicapped child must discover that his disability does not cancel out or even reduce his essential worth as a person. He needs to learn that human dignity and value do not depend on "normality," but that he is a person of worth and significance, handicap and all. If his parents can help him learn this early in life, he will be able to cope with the inevitable limitations and frustrations he will encounter through life without becoming unduly discouraged. He will not give in too easily or give up too quickly when his goals are distant and hard to reach. He will find it easier to deal with the insensitivity, curiosity, or pity which he may encounter in other people and to ask for and accept help when he needs it, without feeling embarrassed or demeaned by his needs.

Parents must recognize that children have *intellectual* and *social* needs, as well as physical and emotional ones. They need to make friends with other children, to accept and be accepted by others. They need to learn to cooperate with other children, to share toys and games with one another, and to be helpful within the family—even though considerable effort may sometimes need to be used to find tasks by which the handicapped child can make a useful contribution. A part of our sense of self-worth comes from the realization that we have something worthwhile to give to others. Parents who are aware of this need will stretch their imagination to help their handicapped child find ways to give, to share, and to feel needed by other family members.

Children also need to be stimulated by varied experiences, both inside and outside the home: hearing stories, reading books, learning to play games, listening to music, taking care of pets, using tools, helping with household chores—as well as visiting neighborhood stores, parks, going to movies, ball games, concerts, parties, picnics, and church activities. Such experiences are not only enjoyable, they are essential if the child is to grow mentally and socially. Handicapped children are likely to have fewer such experiences than normal children. The child with a handicap may not be taken outside the home as often or as far as the normal youngster; he may not be left with others—relatives, friends, babysitters—as often. Vision or hearing problems may limit his experience of the world around him. Because of his handicap, he may not be read to or played with as frequently as the child who is not handicapped.

Since children who are deprived of such experiences will enter school at a disadvantage, it is important for parents to recognize and respond to this need. Though it requires time, effort, and often no little ingenuity to provide such experiences for the handicapped child, it should not be neces-

sary for him to be mentally impoverished during his forma-
tive years.

In addition to the stimulation that comes through varied
experiences, the child also needs to develop a realistic estimate
of his abilities and limitations. He needs to learn what he can
do and what he cannot, and neither should be allowed to
overshadow the other. Bret, for example, may never play
first violin in the school orchestra or sing in the chorus, but
he may express himself creatively through painting or drawing; he may participate in dramatics by building sets or working as part of the technical crew; or he may gain recognition
on the track team. Jennifer will never take ballet lessons or
be a cheerleader, and her lack of coordination may also keep
her from drawing or painting; but she may prove to be gifted at creative writing or mathematics. Parents will need to
exercise patience and understanding in guiding their children
away from activities that would bring them failure and disappointment, while at the same time encouraging them to
develop abilities and pursue goals that are within their reach.

One way in which the social and intellectual needs of children are satisfied is through play and recreation. To be sure,
this is an important part of life for persons of every age, but
it is especially essential for children since it is one of the major
ways in which they develop physically, socially, and mentally
and begin to learn the skills which will enable them to assume the roles and responsibilities of adult life. As a rule,
handicapped children have fewer opportunities than normal
youngsters for play. The child who is disabled may be unable to run, roller skate, or play store or school with children of his own age group. Parents may be overcautious
about letting him try things which seem too hard for him.
Yet play and recreation are every bit as important for the
handicapped as for the normal child.

Parents must also learn to recognize and respond to their

children's *spiritual* needs. Every child needs to know that he is affirmed, loved, sustained, and cherished by that ultimate reality which religious people call God. Moreover, he needs to realize that his life has an important and meaningful place in God's plan for the world. Because of his disability and the limitations it places on him, the handicapped child may have to struggle harder for this realization than the child who is born without a handicap. At times he may be inclined to look upon himself as a mistake, a fault in the creative process, a result of divine negligence or oversight. He may wonder whether his handicap has left him any useful role to play in life, or whether he must be content to sit on the sidelines as a spectator while others more fortunately endowed fight the battles, bear the burdens, and reap the rewards of the world.

Against this background he needs to learn that, in the Jewish and Christian view of life, God created all that is and called it *good;* that God does not measure the worth of any person's life by the size of his accomplishments, whether educational, social, or vocational; that in the sight of God, his life is valued and treasured *as it is,* with all its limitations; and that no human being, however disabled or dependent he may be, is without something important to contribute to the ongoing life of others. One of the ways in which parents respond to these needs is by sharing with him the affirmations, insights, and practices of their own religious tradition.

Seeking Medical Help

When parents begin actively to reach out for assistance for their handicapped child, the first step they usually take is to secure an adequate diagnosis of their child's condition, together with appropriate care and treatment. They ordinarily begin by consulting their family physician or pediatrician. He may refer them to a specialist in the field of their child's particular disability, or to a clinic or rehabilitation center where their child may be evaluated by a team of specialists. In some rural areas traveling clinics are held periodically for this purpose.

Since the handicapped child often has multiple medical problems, a wide variety of specialists may be called on to treat the child. Children who have deformities or injuries to bones, muscles, or joints may require the services of an orthopedist, physiatrist, or physical therapist. Where the brain or nervous system has been damaged, a neurologist may be needed. Children, such as paraplegics, who are unable to control their bowel and bladder functions, will need to be seen by a urologist, so that urinary infections may be prevented or controlled. A psychiatrist or psychologist may be called upon when the disability brings with it mental and emotional problems. Conditions involving the ears, nose, and throat may need to be treated by an otolaryngologist; vision problems by an ophthalmologist; and such conditions as cleft lip and palate may require the services of a plastic surgeon, orthodontist, or prosthodontist. As a rule, the family physician or pediatrician will coordinate and supervise the child's care and will help the parents select those specialists who may be needed from time to time, or find a suitable clinic, hospital, or rehabilitation center.

Parents will want to choose a physician in whom they have confidence, with whom they are able to communicate freely, and who they feel understands them and the problems they are facing with their child. In choosing such a doctor, they entrust to him the central responsibility for managing their child's medical care, but they share this responsibility with him in numerous ways: by giving him complete information about their child and the background of the handicap; by keeping appointments and following his instructions concerning therapy, medicine, diet, or use of appliances; by calling him whenever they notice any difficulties or irregularities; and by asking questions whenever they are uncertain or do not understand some aspect of the child's handicap or its care.

Parents are sometimes intimidated from asking questions by the physician's professional status, expertise, or technical language. Often they find it hard to keep track of all the things they want to ask their doctor, or the information he gives them. Some parents find it helpful to write down in advance a list of items on which they desire clarification; others have found it advantageous for both parents to see the physician together, so that they can more easily remember all that they need to ask and the answers the doctor gives them. Inadequate communication between parents and their doctor will leave them feeling anxious and uncertain, and may hinder the child's progress unnecessarily.

Parents who do not feel confidence in their physician, or are unable to communicate with him freely, may wish to transfer their child to the care of another physician. Certainly they should be aware that at any time they may request consultation with or referral to another physician. It is much better for the child, his parents, and the doctor to deal with such concerns openly and honestly, than for the parents to be uncertain or dissatisfied with the medical care their child is receiving.

Often the physician will prescribe certain specialized therapies for the handicapped child. These will be initiated and directed by specially trained professional therapists, but the parents will usually be responsible for administering or supervising the therapy regularly in the home. *Physical therapy* may be recommended to strengthen weak muscles, improve flexibility of joints, and overcome lack of coordination or control of body movements. Although it makes use of several methods, a principle means of treatment in physical therapy is exercise. Parents may be instructed in the type of exercise which the handicapped child is to perform and asked to make sure these exercises are carried out daily.

Occupational therapy aims at developing useful skills through play, games, creative arts, and handicrafts. Besides improving the functioning of muscles and joints, it contributes to the child's emotional adjustment by relieving restlessness or boredom; and for older children it may lay the groundwork for vocational training and eventual employment. One very important dimension of occupational therapy is training in what are called "activities of daily living." Many handicapped persons have great difficulty with simple, everyday tasks that the nonhandicapped person scarcely thinks about. Eating, bathing, dressing, toileting, writing, or typing may be enormously complex or even impossible tasks for the disabled child. The therapist helps the child master these essential skills by breaking them down into simple motions which can be learned one at a time, or sometimes by devising alternate means for accomplishing the task. Some children whose hands cannot master the skills of writing are taught to use a typewriter. Other handicapped children, who can neither speak nor write, have been taught to communicate by spelling out words on an alphabet chart. Some severely handicapped persons have learned to type with the help of a stylus attached to a band around their head.

Many handicapped children also need *speech therapy*. Disorders of speech are often found among children with cerebral palsy, impaired hearing, cleft lip and palate, and among those who are mentally retarded. Both physical and emotional factors may be involved in speech disorders, and the speech therapist or pathologist is trained to understand and diagnose these as well as to prescribe measures for their correction.

As in other forms of therapy, the active cooperation of the parents is essential for correcting disorders of speech.

Planning for the Future

Having secured adequate medical care and treatment, parents will want to begin as soon as possible to make realistic plans for their child's future. Probably the first question to appear on their horizon is that of *education*. Will their handicapped child be able to attend school? What kind of school? How far will he be able to go in school? These are questions that parents consider quite early, even though they may be unable to answer them for some time. Only one of the families whom I interviewed said they hadn't thought yet about their child's educational future, even though the average age of the handicapped children in this group was just over three years. However, half of the parents had been unable to arrive at any conclusions on the question. "We'll just have to wait and see," was a typical response.

If parents are to make intelligent and wise decisions concerning the education of their handicapped child, they need several things. One is an accurate estimate of the child's limitations and potentialities—physical, mental, and emotional. Some of this may be provided by medical diagnosis and evaluation. Often, however, psychological testing will be needed to determine the child's intelligence and to see whether or not there are any special emotional or perceptual disorders which may affect his ability to learn. This may be done in a medical center or clinic, or perhaps through the local school system.

Because they want so much for him to do well in school, it is easy for parents to overestimate their child's ability. However, it is important not to do so, for the child who is placed in a learning environment where he cannot meet the expectations will be continually frustrated and unhappy.

Yet it is equally important that the child's ability not be *under*estimated. For example, an *educable* mentally retarded child (IQ 50–75) placed in a school for *trainable* youngsters (IQ 25–50) will not be stimulated or challenged sufficiently to develop his full potential. The tragedy of underestimating the capacity of a handicapped child can be seen vividly in the case of a fifty-year-old man whom I was called to see in my role as a hospital chaplain. The man had been born deaf; and although he had been loved and cared for by his parents in their farm home, no attempt had ever been made to teach him to speak, read, or write. Essentially unable to communicate with other human beings except by the most rudimentary gestures, he was at one and the same time almost completely isolated from and yet totally dependent on others. One can only wonder how productive and satisfying a life this person might have been able to live had opportunities been provided for learning when he was a child.

Parents also need to know what educational facilities and resources are available to them and their child. Such information can usually be obtained from their local board of education office or from their state department of education. The educational needs of handicapped children may be met in a number of different ways. Some may attend regular public school classes, with such special provisions as a seat near the teacher's desk or blackboard for the child whose vision or hearing is impaired, or an excuse from physical education or time off for therapy for the physically handicapped child. Other children may attend special classes for the handicapped or retarded which are held in a regular school, so that they are able to associate with nonhandicapped children on the playground and in the lunchroom and still receive the special attention they need in the classroom. The child whose disability is still more severe may be better served in a special day school for the handicapped, where more extensive services and resources are available. Here the environment is more sheltered, and the child will not have to compete with non-handicapped children outside the classroom. Some children may participate in an educational program in a hospital, while others may receive instruction at home, through a visiting tutor, or through radio, television, or telephone contact with the school. Finally, some handicapped children will need to be placed in a residential or boarding school. Among these may be youngsters who are deaf, or blind; those who are severely retarded or who have serious emotional problems; and those who for one reason or another impose severe stress on the family or are disruptive of home life.

One example of a multifaceted approach to the education of the handicapped child can be seen in the University of Iowa Hospital School. Founded in 1948, the school seeks to provide a program of education, care, and treatment for selected handicapped children who cannot be adequately served in their home community; to provide specialized training for prospective workers with physically handicapped or mentally retarded persons; and to foster research into the causes, prevention, and management of handicapping conditions in childhood. In addition to a day school for approximately 90 mentally retarded children who live in the surrounding area, the school has an in-patient unit which provides residential care for approximately 60 physically handicapped children.

> The aim is to rehabilitate these children sufficiently through special education and treatment so that eventually they may return to their home community for the continuance of appropriate management. . . . A comprehensive program of special help is available in the field of medical, dental, and nursing care;

communication skills; various therapies; special education; physical education; industrial arts; homemaking; music; and in child development. Thorough initial and recurrent evaluations of handicapped children are provided on an outpatient basis prior to admission of the child to this section. Through this activity an attempt is made to give parents pertinent instructions regarding care of their child at home and to focus attention on *all* of the child's problems, insofar as possible. *(Annual Report,* University Hospital School, June 30, 1967)

Children who are in-patients at the school range from under three through twenty years in age, and remain there for varying lengths of time. At the nursery level, children may stay for only two to three weeks each time they are admitted, while high-school youngsters are likely to live continuously at the school except for vacation periods, when they return home. Approximately two-thirds of those admitted as in-patients are handicapped by cerebral palsy.

The report just quoted affords a glimpse of the variegated educational prospects for handicapped children. During its first 20 years the school admitted 629 children as in-patients. At the end of that time, nearly one-fourth of these were either pursuing or had completed their education through regular school classes, some of them at the college level. Almost half the group was receiving some form of special education, either in special schools or treatment centers (139), at the Hospital School itself (96), in state schools for the deaf, blind, or mentally retarded (59), or at home (10). About one-sixth of these persons were being cared for at home, some having received the maximum rehabilitation possible for them. The remaining members of the group were either deceased or their educational status was unknown.

Perhaps the most difficult questions parents have to face are, "Will we be able to raise our child at home? Would he be better off in an institution? What effect will his handicap have on our family life?" These are complex issues which each family must resolve for itself; no one can lay down general rules which will apply to all families.

There may be a number of good reasons for placing a child in an institution. Some children need the special therapy or educational program which can only be provided by a residential facility, such as a school for the blind or the deaf. Others may have handicaps so severe that home care is impracticable. Children who are so severely retarded mentally that they are totally dependent on others for feeding, bathing, and diapering, may be able to benefit only from lifetime custodial care. In some cases, the presence of the handicapped child may disrupt family life and impose unwarranted stress on the relationship between husband and wife or between parents and other children. Sometimes the care of the handicapped child becomes more and more difficult as both he and his parents grow older. As they face the prospect of their own declining strength and the likelihood that the child will outlive them, institutional care may present itself as the only realistic alternative.

Parents are likely to approach such a decision with feelings that are both strong and quite mixed. Along with the prospect of relief from the burden of care for the child, there may be varying degrees of guilt, a sense of failure, and sadness over the separation. It is important that parents who are faced with such a decision have the opportunity to think it through carefully, and to express their feelings about it honestly to someone—a physician, social worker, or pastor—who will listen with understanding and respect, and who will assist them in finding the solution to their problem that seems most appropriate to *them*. When a child is to be placed in an institution for care or education, it is important that he be prepared for it as far in advance as possible, and that the decision be interpreted to him in such a way that he does not feel rejected or abandoned, but that he understands as best he can that this step is being taken because his parents love him and want what is best for him.

A number of other areas need to be considered as parents plan for their handicapped child's future. How are his needs for *play, recreation,* and *social activities* to be met? What kinds of activities can he enjoy, within the limitations of his handicap? What toys, equipment, or materials does he need? With whom should he play—other handicapped children, or nonhandicapped children? Are there special social or recreational opportunities of which he could take advantage, such as a day camp for handicapped youngsters? Play is an essential part of the life of every child, and it is important that the handicapped child not be deprived of enjoyable and creative leisure time activity. Learning to relate to other children of his age is also vital, and parents must take care that the handicapped child is not isolated from other children by his disability.

Vocational planning needs to begin early, so that interests and aptitudes may be discovered, opportunities for employment identified, and necessary skills begin to be developed. Although some handicapped persons will never be able to hold gainful employment, others can be employed in sheltered workshops, and an increasing number are finding employment in economically competitive situations. Vocational counseling may be sought through the public schools, a rehabilitation center, or through a state or local office of the Vocational Rehabilitation Administration of the U.S. Department of Health, Education, and Welfare.

Parents must also give thought to the *social and sexual development* of their handicapped child. For some handicapped persons, dating and marriage will simply be out of the question. For many others, however, they are a possibility which cannot be ruled out, and for which careful preparation and guidance is needed. Both those who may marry and those who cannot, need—like nonhandicapped youngsters—the help of parents and teachers to understand, accept, and manage their sexual feelings and impulses.

Finally, the *spiritual and religious development* of the handicapped child needs to be considered carefully. How are parents to share with the child those beliefs, values, and meanings which give their own life order and direction? How are they to transmit to him the religious heritage which claims their loyalty?

Many handicapped children will be able to receive religious instruction in regular classes in their synagogue, church, or parochial school, though in some cases special arrangements may need to be made similar to those in the public school. Parents will want to inform their child's teacher and the superintendent or administrator of the school about his special needs and problems when he is enrolled. Other children, however, may be unable to adjust to the environment of a regular class, or to keep up with the pace of their nonhandicapped classmates. They may need a more sheltered environment, or special equipment or procedures which are not found in the regular classroom. Such children would be better enrolled in a special class.

Where can such special classes for the religious instruction of handicapped persons be found? A few congregations may be large enough to sponsor such classes within their own membership, but for most this is impractical. Not only is the number of handicapped persons in a single church or synagogue likely to be relatively small, but it is apt to include persons of widely varying ages and disabilities, such as blindness, deafness, mental retardation, and cerebral palsy.

In some communities, churches have cooperated in sponsoring classes for persons who are physically handicapped or mentally retarded. This may be done by several churches of the same denomination, or by churches of different denominations, or, as in some areas, through a state or local council of churches. A number of agencies which publish materials for religious instruction have developed curriculum materials for use with handicapped children.

Such learning takes place in several ways. The sharing of words, ideas, and symbols is important. This might seem to be an ineffective approach for handicapped children, especially for those who are mentally retarded. Yet it has been shown that even mentally retarded youngsters believe in and understand God on their own level; and no one who has ever attended a service of worship planned especially for retarded persons can deny their enjoyment of songs and Bible stories or their ability to share sincerely in brief prayers. Only those who are so profoundly retarded that they can receive only custodial care are completely unable to benefit from this kind of teaching. However, in addition to learning through words, ideas, and symbols, children also learn through activities and relationships. A child first experiences the love of God through the love of his parents; he learns that God is faithful as he experiences the trustworthiness and dependability of his mother and father. He learns that there are limits to his behavior—the "moral law"—through the limits which they set for him. He comes to understand grace or forgiveness by their acceptance of him when he has overstepped those limits. He experiences the joy of giving by being allowed to share with others in the family circle. It is through his relationships that the child develops (or fails to develop) what Erik Erikson has called the sense of *basic trust,* which underlies the capacity for genuine faith.

Using Community Resources

As parents reach out for help for their handicapped child, they will also want to discover what resources for assistance are available to them and to their child. Some of this assistance will take the form of medical, educational, or financial aid. Every state has a governmental agency which provides medical services for handicapped children, as well as a program of vocational rehabilitation, both of which are supported by a combination of federal, state, and sometimes local funds. Also, numerous national and local voluntary organizations offer a wide range of assistance to the handicapped person, including diagnostic and treatment services at no or reduced cost; financial aid for treatment or medication; transportation, day care, recreational programs and camping opportunities; special educational programs, counseling, and vocational training; physical aids such as braces, artificial limbs, hearing aids, wheelchairs, record players, and books in Braille; and information, education and counseling for parents. Almost all hospitals, clinics, or rehabilitation centers will have a social worker on the staff who can help parents investigate and make use of the resources that are available in their own area. A social worker may also be found in the offices of a local family service agency.

One sometimes hears the parent of a handicapped child exclaim, "No one can really understand who has not had to face this problem himself!" For this reason, parents often receive as much help from talking with other parents of handicapped children as from talking with professionals. Some clinics and treatment centers conduct group counseling sessions for the parents of children who are seen there. Also, a number of national organizations for the handicapped sponsor local chapters where families may meet regularly and discuss their common problems (and solutions). Examples of such are the National Society for Crippled Children and Adults, the United Cerebral Palsy Association, and the National Association for Retarded Citizens. Such groups can provide mutual understanding and support and thus enable parents to overcome the sense of isolation that sometimes afflicts those whose child is handicapped.

A list of national organizations and governmental agencies that provide help to handicapped persons and their families will be found on pages 101-103 of this book. The parent who does not know where to turn for help may write to the national office of the organization concerned with his child's disability and request information about resources for assistance in his own community and region. No family need feel reluctant or embarrassed to make full use of help that is often readily available to parents who are struggling to help their child grow and develop his full potential as a human being.

5

Sharing
the
Burden

A Family Affair

A further concern which appears as parents reach out for help for their handicapped child is, "How do we relate to others?" This issue is experienced first within the family itself, between the mother and father. A number of studies have indicated that the presence of a retarded or handicapped child may have an adverse effect on the parents' marriage. One investigator believed that a primary cause of marital conflict among families he studied was the need of the handicapped child for special care. Examples of this need which could be cited include the special therapy, handling, and educational equipment often required by the child; the centering of family life around the handicapped child; occasional neglect by the mother of her husband and other children because of the extreme demands of the handicapped child on her time and attention; and the decision of some families to move in order to secure better medical care for their child.[8]

However, the marriage relationship may be a source of strength as well as of conflict. Less than a fifth of the parents in my own study believed that the presence of their handicapped child had produced a strain on their marriage, and more than a third felt they had been drawn closer together as a result of the common problems and responsibilities they shared concerning their child. Further, when asked in whom they confided when worried or perplexed about their child, more than half the parents named their spouse—a response which I had not anticipated. A number of the parents voiced strong appreciation for the support they received from their marriage partner in the task of caring for their disabled child.

Other family relationships may be affected also. The brothers and sisters of the disabled child may suffer from the extraordinary amount of time and attention which the parents devote to his care and therapy. Family outings and activities may be curtailed because the handicapped child is unable to participate. The expenses of medical treatment, therapy, or special education may be so great that other children in the family are denied such things as music lessons, summer camps, and the like. It is important that parents find ways to meet the legitimate needs of *all* the children in the family; the disabled child cannot *always* receive preferential treatment. Sometimes parents must use considerable imagination to find ways of "equalizing" the attention given the handicapped child and his brothers and sisters, so that the latter do not feel neglected and resentful or develop a "martyr" attitude.

Members of the extended family may be helpful, or they may be difficult for parents to deal with. When asked about the attitude of grandparents toward their child's handicap, parents interviewed by the author described some positive aspects such as "concerned," "supportive," "noninterfering," "accepting." However, negative attitudes were mentioned almost twice as often: some grandparents found it hard to accept the handicap, others were overindulgent or overprotective toward the child, and some showed shame, embarrassment, pity, or anxiety concerning the child. "Why does he

have to do those exercises when they hurt him so much?"
"I can't see that the doctors at that clinic are doing her one
bit of good—she still can't walk!" "I think if you just
don't worry, give him more time, he'll be all right." How to
interpret the information and advice they received from medical specialists to grandparents seemed to be a frequent problem for these parents.

What Do We Tell Others?

"How do we answer the children next door who keep asking why Sally doesn't go to school? What should I have
said to that lady in the supermarket who looked at her and
said, 'Poor thing! She can't walk, can she?' " Each family
has to develop its own way of coping with incidents such as
these. As a group parents of handicapped children are extremely sensitive and quick to be offended by attitudes which
they perceive as "curiosity" or "pity." What seems to offend
them most is the large element of superiority that is implied
in the attitude of "feeling sorry for" the parents or their
child. To be the object of someone else's sorrow or pity re-
duces one's own sense of dignity and self-respect. A well-
known poet once remarked, "You know why your friends
come to see you when you're in the hospital? It's not to
comfort you or cheer you up. It's because they're so glad
it's you there and not them!" If a friend, neighbor or relative is motivated primarily by the feeling, "Thank God that's
not my child!" neither the parents nor the child are likely to
experience the relationship as helpful.

However, some parents are hypersensitive to curiosity and
pity, and may imagine them when the other person is merely
expressing genuine concern. Such parents may still be struggling with their own feelings of shame, embarrassment, or

inferiority at having produced a defective child. One mother said, "I never sit down and discuss this with neighbors. If they ask me how Debbie is doing, I tell them O.K. I don't want their opinions." Another said of her daughter, "I'm not ashamed of her—not ashamed to take her with me. There's no reason to be ashamed. I'm proud of her. I wouldn't hide or disown her." But the vehemence of her protest suggests that feelings of shame were just beneath the surface!

Different parents find different ways of coping with these feelings. In one family, the father and mother had devised almost opposite strategies for managing feelings that were quite similar. The father talked freely about his daughter's handicap whenever he had the opportunity. "It's obvious that something is wrong with her," he explained. "I'd rather have people ask about her and know what's wrong than feel sorry for her." But the mother used a different tactic. "I take the position that we don't have to explain our daughter to anybody," she said. Both parents seemed to be coping successfully with their feelings about their child's disability by these different approaches.

"The Thompsons asked me yesterday if there was any way they could help us with Jamie. I didn't know what to say. What should I tell them?" Sometimes friends and neighbors feel a desire to help the family whose child is handicapped, but are held back by a sense of inadequacy at not knowing what to do or a reluctance to "interfere." In some instances persons close to the family have learned to assist in the daily therapy prescribed for the handicapped child, have helped care for other children in the family while parents make necessarily frequent trips to the clinic with the child who is handicapped, or have provided transportation for the child to and from the treatment center or special school.

Some parents struggle so much with their own feelings

about their child's handicap that they misunderstand the interest and concern of others, and avoid or reject offers of help. Such persons feel an intense need to handle their problems by themselves, to "stand on their own feet" and not depend on anyone for help, except perhaps medical and other professional workers. When asked whether the members of her church had offered to help in the care of her child, one such mother replied,

> I don't expect them to. I feel that when you go to people like this, then they feel sorry for you. I don't want people feeling sorry for me.

Such an attitude may be understandable, but it is also unfortunate. It not only deprives the family of what could be much-needed assistance, it also deprives friends and neighbors of the opportunity to share the family's burden, and tends to isolate the family from relationships which they need now more than ever.

What kind of relationships do parents of handicapped children find helpful? In general, they seem to appreciate most those friends and neighbors who show *interest* and *concern* in them and their child, *without condescension.* They value those relationships in which acceptance and understanding are communicated. In such an atmosphere they may feel free from time to time to take the risk of expressing some of the painful feelings they experience in relation to their child —disappointment, perplexity, shame, anger—as well as their positive feelings of affection, gratitude, pride, hope, and love. Such feelings are not fixed and static, but fluid and in a state of constant change. Generally, parents draw strength from friends and neighbors who can allow them to have their own feelings and be just what they are in the present moment, without trying to change them, give them advice,

solve their problems, or make their sometimes difficult decisions for them. What they usually experience as helpful is
not advice, solutions, or decisions, but understanding and
support as they struggle with the problems and opportunities
that confront them and their child.

The Community of Faith

The church or synagogue may be an important source of
help for the family whose child is handicapped. Regular worship may help to sustain the morale of a family under great
stress. The active care and concern of fellow-believers may
provide a community of acceptance in which feelings of
grief, guilt, or resentment may be resolved. Religious teachings may stress the potential meaning and value which can be
won through suffering and loss, and so maintain hope and
faith. An understanding minister can offer invaluable support and guidance as parents work their way through the
long and difficult process of adapting to their child's handicap.

What can a family whose child is handicapped expect from
a pastoral counselor? Such a family has much in common
with other families, and their spiritual needs are far from
unique. The thing that emerges from my own research as
crucially important is the nature of the family's relationship
with their minister, priest, or rabbi. Those parents who had
found their minister helpful most frequently reported no
specific thing he had said or done, but simply that he was with
them when they needed him, that they felt he understood and
accepted them, and that they saw him as a person who cared
about them and their child. The experience reported by two
families is suggestive. The parents of a seventeen-year-old
severely handicapped girl reported that their priest visited
regularly, and brought communion to their daughter because

she was unable to attend mass. Asked if they discussed their special problems as parents of a handicapped youngster with him, the mother replied, "We must have, though I wasn't aware of it at the time." They felt he showed "quite a lot" of understanding of them and their problems, in contrast to his predecessor, who "acted as though he wished we didn't have Diane around."

Similarly, the mother of a handicapped boy contrasted the attitude of her former minister with that of her present pastor.

> When we needed help most, the minister let us down. We were attending church regularly, and the minister would come often to call. He would sit there and tap his foot, say, "Let us pray," and be halfway to the car by the time his wife got her hands unclasped. His relations with people were very stiff and formal. He preached beautiful sermons, but his visits were nothing.

Her response to her current pastor was quite different.

> He's a nut. He sits down and drinks coffee and we argue about why I feel this way. But he's not handing me any answers—he's trying to help me find them myself. I respect him for not giving me answers. But he's *there,* and I appreciate that.

The family that is looking to a minister for help, then, can expect first of all that he will communicate his concern for them within the context of an accepting and understanding relationship and that he will demonstrate his availability to them by regular and frequent contacts. This will be even more likely to happen if they have come to know, respect, and trust him *before* the child's birth or the discovery of its handicap. The family which has a meaningful, ongoing relationship with their minister will be able to receive even more significant help from him when they are confronted by a crisis.

Families may also expect their minister to help them through his preaching and teaching to prepare for unexpected and painful crises in their lives. A number of parents reported that their previous religious training proved to be of great value in helping them deal with the experience of having a child who was handicapped. The meaning of experiences of pain, loss, and suffering forms an essential part of the teaching of most religious traditions. The values, beliefs, and expectations that are formed gradually over a period of years appear to play an important role in determining the manner in which an individual or a family responds to sudden stress. It is, for example, much easier for parents to believe that God does not send disabling conditions upon children in order to punish their parents if they have dealt with this issue over an extended period of time through sermons, Bible classes, or discussion groups, than if they are confronted by it in the moment they discover their child is handicapped.

The expectations we have been discussing relate to needs that are general rather than specific. They are not essentially different from the needs of any person or family in the congregation. However, the family of the handicapped child also has some special needs that set it apart from other families. Its members can expect that their spiritual adviser will be alert and sensitive to these and will be ready to assist them as they seek to fulfill these needs.

The first of these is the need to *resolve feelings of grief* concerning the child's handicap. We have already seen how the experience of having a child who is handicapped may be similar to the loss of a loved one (see Chapter 2). The successful resolution of the crisis of bereavement is usually seen to include three important tasks:

1. The reality of loss and separation from the deceased person must be accepted fully.

2. Painful memories and feelings associated with the person who has been lost must be faced, experienced, and shared with others.

3. Gradually, the bereaved person must withdraw his feelings from the relationship now broken by death, and must reinvest them in new relationships and activities.

Similarly, the parent who is "bereaved" by the discovery that his child is handicapped must also accomplish three tasks:

1. The reality of the handicap must be fully accepted; the child's actual limitations, his deviation from "normality" must be faced.

2. The painful feelings which have been aroused—disappointment and loss, guilt, anger and resentment—must be experienced and shared with other persons.

3. The parents' expectations and desires for a "perfect" child must be relinquished, and their feelings must be reinvested in the actual, handicapped child.

In both kinds of "grief," the pastoral counselor may play an important supportive role, by offering the kind of relationship in which the bereaved person has the opportunity to release and express the painful feelings he is experiencing, and by making available the resources of religious faith to facilitate completion of the mourning process.

However, the family of the handicapped child faces two difficulties that are not present in the usual grief situation. First, the loss in this kind of bereavement is not so open and easily identifiable as when death occurs. The child who has been "lost" and the child who must take the place of the "lost" child are one and the same. Second, in actual bereavement the mourner goes through a well-defined, public ritual, the funeral, which helps to structure his experience and provides a large measure of social acceptance and support. However, for the family of the child who is handicapped, there are no public, socially-accepted rites which correspond to the funeral; their grief is likely to be hidden, private, and inarticulate.

They may find it helpful, then, if their minister can construct or adapt an appropriate ritual to symbolize the meaning of this event for them. If the family belongs to a religious tradition which practices infant baptism, the baptismal service may be modified so as to serve this function. If the family does not belong to such a tradition, or if the child was baptized before the disability was discovered, some other means may need to be found. Perhaps a brief service of thanksgiving and dedication may be held at an appropriate time for family members and close friends, in which the child's handicap is acknowledged, the child himself accepted as God's gift to the family, and in which the parents dedicate themselves to fulfilling, with God's help, the task of caring for this child.

The parents of a child who is handicapped may also expect their minister to be alert and sensitive to any *feelings of shame and inferiority* which they may have. They may find it difficult to express these openly and directly, for in addition to their feelings of shame about their child, many parents also feel ashamed of being ashamed! Where such feelings exist, the pastor may encourage family members to express their feelings more openly, without blame or criticism. If they can allow him, he may also help them search for the sources of these feelings, perhaps in their own sense of inadequacy or wounded pride. He can encourage and support them in attempting to be as open as possible with other persons about their child's special needs and problems. In some instances he may be able to function as a kind of interpreter between the family and other persons in the church or community, to facilitate better understanding. For example, he may enable the parents to accept a certain amount of curiosity about their child on the part of others as normal and natural; and he may help well-meaning persons in the church or community become aware of the revulsion which parents of the handicapped feel toward "pity."

Some parents find it necessary to wrestle with the *meaning of the handicap*. They can expect their minister to be alert to any signals that this is a significant issue for them, and to help them work it through. The question, "Why did this happen to us?" cannot be dealt with solely or even primarily on an intellectual or doctrinal level. It is more than a request for a rational explanation; for many persons it assumes the dimensions of anguished protest, and it may carry a heavy load of guilt or resentment that parents are unable to express directly and openly. The answer to it, therefore, may come more readily through the emotional catharsis of "grief work" than through biblical instruction or theological analysis. However, for some parents the question does have an intellectual dimension which can hardly be ignored.

How can parents expect their pastor to help them as they struggle with this question? They can expect that he will not impose *his own* answer on what is really *their* question, but that with respect for their individuality he will guide them as they search for an answer that makes sense to *them*. They can expect him to share his own insights and convictions freely with them, but to do so in a way that leaves them free to accept or reject these themselves. They can expect his own contributions to the dialogue between them to be carefully timed and adjusted to their own pace. Although he may find it necessary to correct misunderstandings of religious teachings, or to suggest alternative ways to viewing the problem that have not occurred to the parents, he will probably refrain from making authoritative pronouncements. For example, the parent who says, "I just don't understand why God causes children to be born like this!" may experience more help from a response such as "It's awfully difficult to accept something so painful as this," than by a rejoinder like, "Come now, you mustn't go around blaming God for this!"

Since the phrase, "the will of God" has such widely different meanings for different parents, they should not be surprised if their minister is especially careful in his use of these words. He may not want to affirm that their child's handicap is God's will lest he "fix" feelings of guilt or resentment in a religious framework. On the other hand, he may not want to deny that the child's handicap is the will of God lest he deprive the parents of a sense of divine purpose that will give them both strength and hope. He may wish rather to allow them the freedom to arrive at their own answer to this particular question and to understand and respect the meaning their answer carries for them.

Some parents may want help in locating religious resources which provide meaning, direction, and support, and they can expect their minister to suggest certain passages of Scripture, or to guide them to selections from classics or contemporary religious literature for their meditation, study, and spiritual growth. He may also suggest particular prayers or acts of devotion which he feels will be helpful to the family. They can expect him in his concern for the catharsis of painful feelings, not to overlook their need for comfort, encouragement and inspiration.

Support for the task of parenthood is another area of special need for many families of handicapped children. Being a parent is at best an exacting and perplexing role. It is doubly so for the parent whose child is disabled. The care of the child is apt to make heavier demands on the time, energy, and patience of the parents than that of a normal child. Further, parents often have difficulty knowing just what to expect of a child who is handicapped. In the early years of childhood they must live with a considerable measure of uncertainty regarding their child's future, and because they lack any readily available standard for comparison, they may have difficulty establishing adequate and realistic goals for their child. For many families there is the additional problem of how to provide adequate care for the handicapped child without neglecting the legitimate needs of his brothers and sisters. For this reason, the family can expect their pastor to help them find motivation, direction, and support for the continuing tasks of parenthood. They can expect him to exercise a sustaining form of care through his ongoing relationship with them, and to make available to them such religious resources as the support, understanding, and assistance of other persons in the church; classes or discussion groups dealing with family living; devotional readings or practices for use in the home; and any other relevant aspects of the religious tradition which they share. In this connection, the minister may want to explore with the parents the significance of the religious symbol of *vocation* for illumining the tasks and responsibilities of parenthood. A number of parents interviewed by the author found meaning in the belief that their handicapped child was a special task to which God had called them. The minister may wish to support this belief among those who can accept it, and to help them extend it to include their non-handicapped children as well.

The need for referral is another to which a family may expect their spiritual adviser to remain alert. He will seldom be the first person to whom they turn for help for their handicapped child. and it is unrealistic to expect him to have a detailed knowledge of the many conditions that are responsible for childhood handicaps, for he will encounter any one of them only occasionally, if at all. Yet they can expect him to have at hand some information which will enable him to direct persons who have special needs and problems toward other appropriate sources of professional help. The minister who is working with a family that is concerned that their child may be handicapped may urge them to consult their own physician or pediatrician, or he may suggest a nearby medical center with adequate diagnostic facilities. He may also wish to refer the family for other needed services to educational, family services, mental health, or rehabilitation agencies.

As they learn to share their burden with one another, with other family members, with concerned and understanding friends and neighbors, with fellow-believers and a minister in whom they have confidence, parents of a handicapped child may come to realize that they do not have to fulfill their perplexing responsibilities alone, but that there are others who care with and for them; and above all, an Other who gives purpose and hope to their efforts, and on whose strength they may draw when their task is difficult and demanding.

Notes

1. Ray H. Barsch, *The Parent of the Handicapped Child* (Springfield, Illinois: Charles C. Thomas, 1968), p. 92.

2. Albert Solnit and Mary Stark, "Mourning and the Birth of a Defective Child," *The Psychoanalytic Study of the Child*, XVI (1961), p. 532.

3. Helen Wortis and William Cooper, "The Life Experience of Persons with Cerebral Palsy," *American Journal of Physical Medicine*, XXXVI, No. 6 (1957), pp. 328-344.

4. Barsch, p. 339.

5. Charles E. Palmer, *Religion and Rehabilitation*. (Springfield, Illinois: Charles C. Thomas, 1968), pp. 47-48.

6. David B. Ray, *A Study to Develop a Guide of Education for Parents of Cerebral Palsied Children*, M.A. Thesis, (Iowa City, State University of Iowa, 1951), pp. 26, 27.

7. Barsch, p. 292.

8. Glenn Boles, "Personality Factors in Mothers of Cerebral Palsied Children," *Genetic Psychology Monographs*, LXIX (May 1959), pp. 212-213.

For
Further
Help

Two kinds of resources are included in this section for persons who desire further information. The first is a brief, annotated list of books which may be of interest to parents, ministers, teachers, and other interested persons. The second is a list of some national organizations and governmental agencies which provide help to handicapped persons and their families.

Books

Ayrault, Evelyn West. *You Can Raise Your Handicapped Child*. New York: G. P. Putnam's Sons, 1964.

As the title suggests, this is a realistic but hopeful and encouraging book for parents, written by a professionally trained person who has herself experienced the difficulties of which she writes. It shows keen insight into the feelings of both children and parents, and is enriched by the generous use of case material.

Barsch, Ray H. *The Parent of the Handicapped Child*. Springfield: Charles C. Thomas, 1968.

This book reports the results of a wide-ranging study of the perceptions, attitudes, and child-rearing practices of the parents of 177 children handicapped by blindness, deafness, mongolism, cerebral palsy, and brain injury. One chapter deals with the role of religion in the life of the families. The author found no evidence that the parents had buried themselves in social isolation as a result of their child's handicap, and believes that the general tendency to describe parents of handicapped children as guilt-ridden, anxious, overprotective and rejecting is simply not true.

Buck, Pearl. *The Child Who Never Grew.* New York: John Day Co., 1950.

This is the poignant and moving account by a famous novelist of her discovery that her own daughter was mentally retarded, her subsequent search for help, and her eventual decision to place the child in an institution for care.

Cruickshank, William M., ed. *Cerebral Palsy: Its Individual and Community Problems.* Revised edition. Syracuse: Syracuse University Press, 1966.

An excellent and comprehensive treatment of one major handicapping condition, this book contains chapters by various authorities on the medical aspects of cerebral palsy; its effect on intelligence and personality; speech, language, hearing, and visual problems; physical and occupational therapy; educational and vocational planning; parent counseling, social casework, and total community planning.

The Directory for Exceptional Children. Seventh edition. Boston: Porter Sargent, 1972.

This valuable reference book contains a listing of private and public schools, clinics, treatment centers, and residential and day-care facilities in the United States and Canada for children who are emotionally disturbed or socially maladjusted, mentally retarded, deaf or hard of hearing, and for those who have orthopedic, neurological, visual, or speech handicaps. Institutions are listed by the type of handicap served and by state. Information is given for each on the nature of the program, administration and professional staff, the kind of children and handicaps served, rates, and sponsoring or controlling agency. The *Directory* also lists associations, societies, foundations, and state and federal agencies concerned directly or indirectly with the welfare of handicapped or exceptional children.

Kvaraceus, William C. and E. Nelson Hayes. *If Your Child Is Handicapped*. Boston: Porter Sargent, 1969.

A collection of autobiographical reports from parents of handicapped children, showing how some parents have faced and tried to solve their problems. It includes contributions from parents of children who are cerebral palsied and orthopedically handicapped, mentally retarded, deaf and hard of hearing, blind and partially sighted, emotionally disturbed, and who have special health problems.

Lewis, C. S. *The Problem of Pain*. New York: The Macmillan Company, 1943.

A classic work by the well-known British author on the religious meaning of suffering, this book views the possibility of suffering as an inherent consequence of natural order and of human freedom. The author sees the purpose of pain as essentially remedial and redemptive: its function is to shatter our comfortable illusion of self-sufficiency, to bring us to the recognition that something is radically wrong with our lives, and so provide the opportunity for repentance and reconciliation with God.

Neufeld, John, *Touching*. New York: S. G. Phillips, 1970.

This book is a sensitive, insightful, and beautifully-written novel for young readers about a sixteen-year-old cerebral palsied girl and her family.

Noland, Robert, ed. *Counseling Parents of the Ill and the Handicapped*. Springfield: Charles C. Thomas, 1971.

A collection of articles and papers from various professional

journals dealing with the problems of parents of the handicapped. It includes sections on mental retardation; epilepsy
and cerebral palsy; speech, hearing, and visual handicaps;
cardiac, diabetic, hemophiliac, and asthmatic conditions; severe and terminally ill children; and genetic counseling. A
helpful resource for the pastor or other professional working
with a family whose child is handicapped.

Palmer, Charles E. *The Church and the Exceptional Person.*
   Nashville: Abingdon Press, 1961.

This small book is intended to help churches reach out to
handicapped or gifted persons in the community and include
them in their fellowship and ministry. It contains much
practical information on designing and planning programs
for the exceptional person and gives brief and accurate descriptions of the most common handicapping conditions.

Palmer, Charles E. *Religion and Rehabilitation.* Springfield:
   Charles C. Thomas, 1968.

Written by a well-known professional worker in the field
of rehabilitation, this book stresses the potential contribution of religion to the rehabilitation process. The author
sees religion as a catalyst which helps disabled persons discover their own untapped resources, sustains their hope, and
strengthens their motivation to cooperate actively in the
therapeutic process.

Spock, Benjamin, and Marion O. Lerrigo. *Caring for Your
   Disabled Child.* New York: The Macmillan Company,
   1965.

Readers who feel the need of a more detailed discussion of
the practical day-to-day problems encountered in raising a
handicapped child will find a helpful resource in this excel-

lent "common-sense" book. My own treatment of the topics in Chapter 4 is indebted to these authors' well-balanced presentation of such issues as medical care and rehabilitation, education, vocational planning, recreation, social and sexual development, and tools and techniques for daily living.

Stubblefield, Harold W. *The Church's Ministry in Mental Retardation*. Nashville: Broadman Press, 1965.

A useful book by a minister who serves as chaplain in an institution for the mentally retarded. Of special interest are his discussion of the theological dimensions of retardation, and a chapter on "The Religious Consciousness of the Retarded." Drawing upon his own research, the author challenges the view that retarded persons lack either religious consciousness or responsibility, and suggests instead that these are present in a degree relative to the mental and chronological development of the individual.

Weatherhead, Leslie. *Why Do Men Suffer?* Nashville: Abingdon Press, 1936.

Another classic, this book is by a popular British preacher who was concerned throughout his career with the relationship between religion, illness, and healing. The author insists that although God permits suffering he does not *intend* it; and places strong emphasis on the reality of God's presence with the sufferer, and his ability to bring good out of evil.

Organizations and Agencies

The following organizations or agencies provide assistance of various kinds to persons who are handicapped. Parents may write for additional information concerning the services available to them or to their child. The asterisk (*) denotes six major national organizations which provide direct services to the handicapped and have chapters in each state.

EMOTIONAL OR SOCIAL DISTURBANCE

*National Association for Mental Health, 1800 North Kent Street, Rosslyn, Arlington, Virginia 22209

Big Brothers of America, 341 Suburban Station Building, Philadelphia, Pennsylvania 19103. Publishes a directory of agencies for socially maladjusted children.

MENTAL RETARDATION

*National Association for Retarded Citizens, 2709 Avenue "E" East, Arlington, Texas 76011

ORTHOPEDIC AND NEUROLOGICAL HANDICAPS

*Association for Children with Learning Disabilities, 2200 Brownsville Road, Pittsburgh, Pennsylvania 15210

*Human Growth Foundation, 307 Fifth Avenue, New York, New York 10016

*National Easter Seal Society for Crippled Children and Adults, 2023 W. Ogden Avenue, Chicago, Illinois 60612

*United Cerebral Palsy Association, Inc., 66 E. 34th Street, New York, New York 10016

Muscular Dystrophy Associations of America, 1790 Broadway, New York, New York 10019

National Multiple Sclerosis Society, 257 Park Avenue South, New York, New York 10010

VISUAL HANDICAPS

American Foundation for the Blind, 15 West 16th Street, New York, New York 10011

American Printing House for the Blind, 1839 Frankfort Avenue, Louisville, Kentucky 40206

John Milton Society, 160 Fifth Avenue, New York, New York
Publishes religious literature and Sunday school lessons.

National Council of State Agencies for the Blind, P.O. Box 12866, Austin, Texas 78711

National Society for the Prevention of Blindness, 79 Madison Avenue, New York, New York 10016

SPEECH AND HEARING HANDICAPS

Alexander Graham Bell Association for the Deaf (Volta Bureau), 3417 Volta Place, NW, Washington, DC 20007

American Speech and Hearing Association, 9030 Old Georgetown Road, Washington, DC 20015

John Tracy Clinic, 806 West Adams Boulevard, Los Angeles, California 90007
Provides a correspondence course for parents of deaf children.

National Association of the Deaf, 814 Thayer Avenue, Silver Spring, Maryland 20910

National Association of Hearing and Speech Agencies (formerly American Hearing Society), 919 18th Street NW, Washington, DC 20006

OTHER

American Camping Association, Bradford Woods, Martinsville, Indiana 46151
Publishes a Directory of Camps for the Handicapped.

American Legion, National Veterans Affairs and Rehabilitation Commission, 1608 K Street, NW, Washington, DC 20006
Provides services for veterans and their children.

American National Red Cross, 17th and D Streets NW, Washington, DC 20006
Instruction in swimming and crafts.

Boy Scouts of America, North Brunswick, New Jersey 08902
Publishes handbooks on scouting for the mentally retarded, physically handicapped, and visually handicapped.

Council for Exceptional Children, 1411 S. Jefferson Davis Highway, Suite 900, Arlington, Virginia 22202

Department of Health, Education and Welfare, Social and Rehabilitation Service, 330 Independence SW, Washington, DC 20201

Girl Scouts of the United States of America, 830 3rd Avenue, New York, New York 10022

Office of Education; Bureau of Education for the Handicapped, Box 19428, Washington, DC 20036
Provides information without charge on services available to children with mental, emotional, and learning handicaps.

Other Titles in the Religion and Medicine Series

GLEN W. DAVIDSON, EDITOR

WHAT CAN I DO ABOUT THE PART OF ME I DON'T LIKE?

"The part of me I don't like" may be a birth defect, physical handicap, speech problem, or a disabling disease. David Belgum helps you understand these personal problems and shows how you can accept and overcome them. *By David R. Belgum, Ph.D., member of the faculties of the School of Religion and the College of Medicine of the University of Iowa.*

UNDERSTANDING MENTAL ILLNESS: A LAYMAN'S GUIDE

A book to help you understand the types of mental illness and their symptoms, professional therapy and how you can help, and the relationship of religion to mental health. *By Nancy C. Andreasen, Ph.D., M.D., assistant professor of psychiatry at the University of Iowa College of Medicine.*

LIVING WITH DYING

Do you know how to help when a friend or relative is dying? Glen Davidson uses latest research to show you how to handle your own emotions, understand the dying, and respond to their needs. *By Glen W. Davidson, Ph.D., Director, Division of Medical Humanities, Southern Illinois University School of Medicine.*